KINGSFORD®

— GREAT — BARBECUES

KINGSFORD

GREAT BARBECUES

Classics

Baby Back Ribs

¼ cup packed brown sugar
2 tablespoons dry mustard
2 teaspoons paprika
2 teaspoons salt
1 teaspoon black pepper

2 racks pork baby back ribs
  (3½ to 4 pounds)
⅓ to ½ cup K.C. Masterpiece
  Original Barbecue Sauce

Combine sugar, mustard, paprika, salt and pepper. Rub mixture evenly onto ribs to coat. Place ribs on covered grill opposite medium Kingsford briquets. Grill 30 to 45 minutes or until tender and cooked through, turning once and brushing with barbecue sauce during last 10 minutes of grilling. *Makes 4 servings*

Nutrients per Serving: Calories: 421, protein: 39 g, fat: 21 g, carbohydrate: 17 g, sodium: 1451 mg, cholesterol: 62 mg

Garlic-Dijon Butterflied Lamb

½ cup red wine vinegar
¼ cup coarse-grained mustard
8 cloves garlic, minced
2 tablespoons minced fresh
  rosemary

1 tablespoon olive oil
½ teaspoon salt
½ teaspoon black pepper
4 pounds butterflied boneless
  leg of lamb

Combine vinegar, mustard, garlic, rosemary, oil, salt and pepper in large glass dish. Add lamb; turn to coat. Cover and refrigerate at least 8 hours or up to 2 days, turning occasionally. Remove lamb from marinade; discard marinade. Grill lamb on covered grill over medium Kingsford briquets about 25 to 30 minutes until thickest portion is medium-rare or to desired doneness, turning 4 times. *Makes 8 to 10 servings*

Nutrients per Serving (¹⁄₁₀ of Garlic-Dijon Butterflied Lamb): Calories: 333, protein: 48 g, fat: 14 g, carbohydrate: 1 g, sodium: 209 mg, cholesterol: 152 mg

Baby Back Ribs

Tandoori-Style Seafood Kabobs

In India, meat and poultry are cooked in an extremely
hot tandoori clay oven. This method cooks food quickly,
charring the outside and leaving the inside moist. Here, seafood
kabobs are grilled over a medium-hot grill for a similar effect.

½ pound *each* salmon fillet,
　　tuna steak and swordfish
　　steak*
1 teaspoon salt
1 teaspoon ground cumin
¼ teaspoon black pepper
　Dash ground cinnamon
　Dash ground cloves
　Dash ground nutmeg
　Dash ground cardamom
　　(optional)
½ cup plain low-fat yogurt
¼ cup lemon juice

1 piece (1-inch cube) peeled
　　fresh ginger, minced
1 tablespoon olive oil
2 cloves garlic, minced
½ jalapeño pepper, seeded
　　and minced
½ pound large shrimp, shelled
　　with tails intact, deveined
1 *each* red and green bell
　　pepper, cut into bite-size
　　pieces
　Fresh parsley sprigs
　Fresh chives

Cut fish into 1½-inch cubes; cover and refrigerate. Heat salt and spices in
small skillet over medium heat until fragrant (or spices may be added to
marinade without heating); place spices in 2-quart glass dish. Add yogurt,
lemon juice, ginger, oil, garlic and jalapeño pepper; mix well. Add fish and
shrimp; turn to coat. Cover and refrigerate at least 1 hour but no longer
than 2 hours. Thread a variety of seafood onto each metal or wooden
skewer, alternating with bell peppers. (Soak wooden skewers in hot water
30 minutes to prevent burning.) Grill kabobs over medium-hot Kingsford
briquets about 2 minutes per side until fish flakes easily when tested with
fork and shrimp are pink and opaque. Remove seafood and peppers from
skewers. Garnish with parsley and chives. 　　　　*Makes 4 servings*

*Any firm fish can be substituted for any fish listed above.

Nutrients per Serving: Calories: 278, protein: 40 g, fat: 11 g, carbohydrate: 3 g,
sodium: 271 mg, cholesterol: 101 mg

Tandoori-Style Seafood Kabob

Jamaican Steak

A sweet blend of orange and lime juices, ginger, garlic, and hints of cinnamon and cloves makes the perfect marinade for flank steak.

2 pounds beef flank steak
¼ cup packed brown sugar
3 tablespoons orange juice
3 tablespoons lime juice
3 cloves garlic, minced
1 piece (1½×1 inches) fresh ginger, minced
2 teaspoons grated orange peel

2 teaspoons grated lime peel
1 teaspoon salt
1 teaspoon black pepper
¼ teaspoon ground cinnamon
⅛ teaspoon ground cloves
Shredded orange peel
Shredded lime peel

Score both sides of beef.* Combine sugar, juices, garlic, ginger, grated peels, salt, pepper, cinnamon and cloves in 2-quart glass dish. Add beef; turn to coat. Cover and refrigerate steak at least 2 hours. Remove beef from marinade; discard marinade. Grill beef over medium-hot Kingsford briquets about 6 minutes per side until medium-rare or to desired doneness. Garnish with shredded orange and lime peels.

Makes 6 servings

*To score flank steak, cut ¼-inch-deep diagonal lines about 1 inch apart in surface of steak to form diamond-shaped design.

Nutrients per Serving: Calories: 283, protein: 30 g, fat: 17 g, carbohydrate: 0 g, sodium: 97 mg, cholesterol: 81 mg

Jamaican Steak

Classic Grilled Chicken

Chicken from the grill is a perfect choice for family or friends. Enjoy this classic recipe alone or serve it with Spicy Peanut Sauce (page 10), Cilantro Salsa (page 10) or Italian Salsa Verde (page 11).

1 whole frying chicken*
   (3½ pounds), quartered
¼ cup lemon juice
¼ cup olive oil
2 tablespoons soy sauce

2 large cloves garlic, minced
½ teaspoon sugar
½ teaspoon ground cumin
¼ teaspoon black pepper

Rinse chicken under cold running water; pat dry with paper towels. Arrange chicken in 13×9×2-inch glass baking dish. Combine remaining ingredients in small bowl; pour half of mixture over chicken. Cover and refrigerate chicken at least 1 hour or overnight. Cover and reserve remaining mixture in refrigerator to use for basting. Remove chicken from marinade; discard marinade. Arrange medium Kingsford briquets on each side of large rectangular metal or foil drip pan. Pour hot tap water into drip pan until half full. Place chicken on grid directly above drip pan. Grill chicken, skin side down, on covered grill 25 minutes. Baste with reserved baste. Turn chicken; cook 20 to 25 minutes or until juices run clear and chicken is no longer pink in center. *Makes 6 servings*

Substitute 3½ pounds of chicken parts for whole chicken, if desired. Grill legs and thighs about 35 minutes and breast halves about 25 minutes or until chicken is no longer pink in center, turning once.

Nutrients per Serving (without skin): Calories: 404, protein: 44 g, fat: 24 g, carbohydrate: 1 g, sodium: 255 mg, cholesterol: 137 mg

Classic Grilled Chicken with
Italian Salsa Verde (page 11)

Spicy Peanut Sauce

⅔ cup canned coconut milk
4 tablespoons sugar*
2 large cloves garlic, minced
1½ teaspoons minced fresh
  ginger

⅛ teaspoon salt
⅛ to ¼ teaspoon cayenne
  pepper
⅓ cup chunky peanut butter
3 tablespoons lemon juice

Combine coconut milk, sugar, garlic, ginger, salt and pepper in 2-quart saucepan; bring to a boil over high heat. Cook over medium heat 5 minutes, stirring occasionally. Stir in peanut butter and lemon juice; cook and stir 3 minutes. If sauce separates or is too thick, stir in 1 to 2 tablespoons boiling water. *Makes about ¾ cup*

If peanut butter contains sugar, decrease sugar to 3 tablespoons.

Nutrients per Serving (3 tablespoons): Calories: 168, protein: 5 g, fat: 15 g, carbohydrate: 6 g, sodium: 115 mg, cholesterol: 0 mg

Cilantro Salsa

2 cups packed cilantro leaves
½ small red onion, coarsely
  chopped
2 tablespoons lemon juice
2 tablespoons water
1 to 2 jalapeño peppers,
  seeded and coarsely
  chopped

¾ teaspoon sugar
½ teaspoon salt
¼ teaspoon black pepper

Combine all ingredients in food processor; process until well blended, scraping sides of bowl several times. Serve at room temperature with grilled chicken, fish, pork or lamb. Refrigerate leftovers.

Makes about 1 cup

Nutrients per Serving (¼ cup): Calories: 15, protein: 0 g, fat: trace, carbohydrate: 3 g, sodium: 271 mg, cholesterol: 0 mg

Italian Salsa Verde

½ cup packed Italian parsley,
 finely chopped
¼ cup olive oil
3 tablespoons lemon juice

2 tablespoons capers, chopped
1 shallot *or* 2 green onions,
 thinly sliced
⅛ teaspoon black pepper

Combine all ingredients in small bowl; let stand about 30 minutes. Serve at room temperature with grilled chicken or fish; refrigerate leftovers.

Makes about ⅔ cup

Nutrients per Serving (about 2½ tablespoons): Calories: 128, protein: 0 g, fat: 15 g, carbohydrate: 2 g, sodium: 162 mg, cholesterol: 0 mg

Perfectly Grilled Steak & Potatoes

Olive oil
1½ teaspoons cracked black
 pepper
2 cloves garlic, pressed
 Salt
½ teaspoon dried thyme leaves
4 beef tenderloin steaks or
 boneless top loin steaks,
 1½ inches thick

4 medium potatoes, cut into
 ½-inch slices
Ground black pepper
Lime wedges

Combine 2 tablespoons oil, cracked pepper, garlic, ½ teaspoon salt and thyme in cup. Brush oil mixture over steaks to coat both sides. Brush potato slices with additional oil; season to taste with additional salt and ground pepper. Lightly oil hot grid to prevent sticking. Grill beef on covered grill over medium-hot Kingsford briquets 10 to 12 minutes for medium-rare or to desired doneness, turning once. Grill potatoes 10 to 12 minutes or until golden brown and tender, turning once. Serve steaks with potatoes and lime wedges.

Makes 4 servings

Nutrients per Serving: Calories: 527, protein: 33 g, fat: 21 g, carbohydrate: 52 g, sodium: 451 mg, cholesterol: 76 mg

Barbecued Salmon

4 salmon steaks,
   ¾ to 1 inch thick
3 tablespoons lemon juice
2 tablespoons soy sauce
   Salt and black pepper

½ cup K.C. Masterpiece
   Original Barbecue Sauce
Fresh oregano sprigs
Grilled mushrooms

Rinse salmon; pat dry with paper towels. Combine lemon juice and soy sauce in shallow glass dish. Add salmon; let stand at cool room temperature no more than 15 to 20 minutes, turning salmon several times. Remove salmon from marinade; discard marinade. Season lightly with salt and pepper.

Lightly oil hot grid to prevent sticking. Grill salmon on covered grill over medium Kingsford briquets 10 to 14 minutes. Halfway through cooking time brush salmon with barbecue sauce, then turn and continue grilling until fish flakes easily when tested with fork. Remove fish from grill; brush with barbecue sauce. Garnish with oregano sprigs and mushrooms.

Makes 4 servings

Nutrients per Serving: Calories: 215, protein: 25 g, fat: 10 g, carbohydrate: 4 g, sodium: 433 mg, cholesterol: 70 mg

Barbecued Salmon

Pork Chops with Apple-Sage Stuffing

The sweetness of apple and the herblike essence of vermouth combine with sage to create a delicious stuffing for pork.

6 center-cut pork chops
(3 pounds), about 1 inch
thick
¾ cup dry vermouth, divided
4 tablespoons minced fresh
sage *or* 4 teaspoons
rubbed sage, divided
2 tablespoons soy sauce
1 tablespoon olive oil
2 cloves garlic, minced

½ teaspoon black pepper,
divided
1 tablespoon butter
1 medium onion, diced
1 apple, cored and diced
½ teaspoon salt
2 cups fresh firm-textured
white bread crumbs
Curly endive
Plum slices

Cut pocket in each chop using tip of thin, sharp knife. Combine ¼ cup vermouth, 2 tablespoons fresh sage (or 2 teaspoons rubbed sage), soy sauce, oil, garlic and ¼ teaspoon pepper in glass dish; add pork chops, turning to coat. Heat butter in large skillet over medium heat until foamy. Add onion and apple; cook and stir about 6 minutes until onion is tender. Stir in remaining ½ cup vermouth, 2 tablespoons sage, ¼ teaspoon pepper and salt. Cook and stir over high heat about 3 minutes until liquid is almost gone. Transfer onion mixture to large bowl. Stir in bread crumbs.

Remove pork chops from marinade; discard marinade. Spoon onion mixture into pockets of pork chops. Close openings with wooden picks. (Soak wooden picks in hot water 15 minutes to prevent burning.) Grill pork chops on covered grill over medium Kingsford briquets about 5 minutes per side until barely pink in center. Garnish with endive and plum slices. *Makes 6 servings*

Nutrients per Serving: Calories: 83, protein: 25 g, fat: 14 g, carbohydrate: 33 g, sodium: 614 mg, cholesterol: 71 mg

Pork Chop with
Apple-Sage Stuffing

Cajun Grilled Shrimp

Frozen shelled and deveined shrimp are a
great time-saver; just thaw and cook them.

3 green onions, minced
2 tablespoons lemon juice
3 cloves garlic, minced
2 teaspoons paprika
1 teaspoon salt
¼ to ½ teaspoon black pepper

¼ to ½ teaspoon cayenne
   pepper
1 tablespoon olive oil
1½ pounds shrimp, shelled with
   tails intact, deveined
Lemon wedges

Combine onions, lemon juice, garlic, paprika, salt and peppers in 2-quart
glass dish; stir in oil. Add shrimp; turn to coat. Cover and refrigerate at
least 15 minutes. Thread shrimp onto metal or wooden skewers. (Soak
wooden skewers in hot water 30 minutes to prevent burning.) Grill
shrimp over medium-hot Kingsford briquets about 2 minutes per side
until opaque. Serve immediately with lemon wedges.

Makes 4 servings

Nutrients per Serving: Calories: 139, protein: 26 g, fat: 3 g, carbohydrate: 1 g,
sodium: 189 mg, cholesterol: 194 mg

Cajun Grilled Shrimp

Entertaining

Garlic-Pepper Skewered Pork

This skewered pork recipe requires only half of a
2½-pound boneless pork loin roast. The remainder of the
roast is cut into chops, marinated, grilled and refrigerated;
use the chops another day to prepare Thai Pork Salad (page 30).

1 boneless pork loin roast
   (about 2½ pounds)
6 to 15 cloves garlic, minced
⅓ cup lime juice
3 tablespoons firmly packed
   brown sugar

3 tablespoons soy sauce
2 tablespoons vegetable oil
2 teaspoons black pepper
¼ teaspoon cayenne pepper
8 green onions, cut into
   2-inch pieces (optional)

Cut pork crosswise into six ½-inch-thick chops, reserving remaining
roast. (Each chop may separate into 2 pieces.) Set chops aside in
13×9×2-inch glass dish. Cut remaining pork roast lengthwise into
2 pieces. Cut each piece into ⅛-inch-thick strips; place in dish with chops.
To prepare marinade, combine all remaining ingredients except green
onions in small bowl. Pour marinade over pork chops and slices; cover
and refrigerate at least 1 hour or overnight. Thread pork slices ribbon
style onto metal skewers, alternating pork with green onions. Grill
skewered pork slices and chops over medium-hot Kingsford briquets
about 3 minutes per side until no longer pink in center. (Chops may
require 1 to 2 minutes longer.) *Do not overcook.* Serve skewered pork
immediately. Cover and refrigerate chops for Thai Pork Salad (page 30).

Makes 4 to 6 servings
(plus 6 chops for Thai Pork Salad)

Nutrients per Serving: (⅙ of recipe): Calories: 247, protein: 23 g, fat: 13 g, carbohydrate: 7 g,
sodium: 425 mg, cholesterol: 73 mg

Garlic-Pepper Skewered Pork

Grilled Paella

1½ to 2 pounds chicken wings
  or thighs
2 tablespoons plus ¼ cup
  extra-virgin olive oil,
  divided
Salt and black pepper
1 pound garlicky sausage
  links, such as linguisa,
  chorizo or Italian
1 large onion, chopped
2 large red bell peppers,
  seeded and cut into thin
  strips
4 cloves garlic, minced

1 can (14 ounces) diced
  tomatoes, undrained
4 cups uncooked rice
16 tightly closed live mussels
  or clams,* scrubbed
½ pound large shrimp,* peeled
  and deveined with tails
  intact
1½ cups frozen peas
1 can (about 14 ounces)
  chicken broth
2 lemons, cut into wedges
1 oval disposable foil pan
  (about 17×13×3 inches)

Brush chicken with 2 tablespoons oil; season with salt and black pepper.
Grill chicken and sausage on covered grill over medium Kingsford
briquets 15 to 20 minutes or until chicken juices run clear and sausage is
no longer pink, turning every 5 minutes. Cut sausage into 2-inch pieces.

Heat remaining ¼ cup oil in large skillet over medium-high heat. Add
onion, bell peppers and garlic; cook and stir 5 minutes or until vegetables
are tender. Add tomatoes, 1½ teaspoons salt and ½ teaspoon black pepper;
cook about 8 minutes until thick, stirring frequently. Combine onion
mixture and rice in foil pan; spread evenly. Arrange chicken, sausage,
seafood and peas over rice. Bring broth and 6 cups water to a boil in
3 quart saucepan. Place foil pan on grid over medium Kingsford briquets;
immediately pour boiling broth mixture over rice. Grill on covered grill
about 20 minutes until liquid is absorbed. *Do not stir.* Cover with foil; let
stand 10 minutes. Garnish with lemon wedges.

Makes 8 to 10 servings

Seafood can be omitted; add an additional 1¼ to 1½ pounds chicken.

Nutrients per Serving (¹⁄₁₀ of recipe): Calories: 572, protein: 26 g, fat: 22 g, carbohydrate: 67 g,
sodium: 875 mg, cholesterol: 82 mg

Grilled Paella

Jamaican Jerk Chicken

⅔ cup chopped green onions
3 tablespoons minced fresh
    thyme leaves *or*
    1 tablespoon dried thyme
    leaves
3 tablespoons peanut oil
3 tablespoons soy sauce
2 tablespoons minced fresh
    ginger
1 tablespoon minced garlic
1 habañero pepper, seeded and
    minced *or* 1 tablespoon
    minced, seeded serrano
    pepper

1 bay leaf
1 teaspoon freshly ground
    black pepper
1 teaspoon whole coriander
½ teaspoon ground nutmeg
½ teaspoon ground allspice
4 skinless boneless chicken
    breast halves (4 to
    6 ounces each)

To prepare marinade, combine all ingredients except chicken in small bowl; mix well. Place chicken in glass dish. Coat chicken with marinade. Marinate in refrigerator, several hours or overnight. Remove chicken from marinade; discard marinade. Grill chicken on covered grill over medium Kingsford briquets 4 to 6 minutes per side or until juices run clear.

Makes 4 servings

Nutrients per Serving: Calories: 226, protein: 23 g, fat: 13 g, carbohydrate: 5 g, sodium: 740 mg, cholesterol: 57 mg

Beef with Dry Spice Rub

3 tablespoons firmly packed
    brown sugar
1 tablespoon black
    peppercorns
1 tablespoon yellow mustard
    seeds
1 tablespoon whole coriander
    seeds

4 cloves garlic
1½ to 2 pounds beef top round
    steak or London Broil,
    about ½ inch thick
Vegetable or olive oil
Salt

Place sugar, peppercorns, mustard seeds, coriander seeds and garlic in blender or food processor; process until seeds and garlic are crushed. Rub beef with oil; pat on spice mixture. Season generously with salt.

Lightly oil hot grid to prevent sticking. Grill beef on covered grill over medium-low Kingsford briquets 16 to 20 minutes for medium or until desired doneness, turning once. Let stand 5 minutes before cutting across the grain into thin diagonal slices. *Makes 6 servings*

Nutrients per Serving: Calories: 249, protein: 29 g, fat: 11 g, carbohydrate: 9 g, sodium: 106 mg, cholesterol: 73 mg

Tuna Tacos with Grilled Pineapple Salsa

Grilled fish topped with fruit salsa has become standard fare at trendy restaurants. This recipe wraps tasty morsels of grilled tuna and a fiery pineapple salsa in corn tortillas for delicious soft tacos.

Tuna Vera Cruz (page 40)
½ large pineapple, peeled, cored and cut into ½-inch thick slices
8 corn tortillas
½ medium red onion, cut into thin slivers
¼ cup cilantro leaves, chopped

1 tablespoon lime juice
1 to 3 teaspoons minced, seeded jalapeño pepper
1 garlic clove, minced
¼ teaspoon salt
¼ teaspoon freshly ground black pepper

Prepare Tuna Vera Cruz; keep warm. Grill pineapple over medium-hot Kingsford briquets about 2 minutes per side until lightly browned. Grill tortillas until hot but not crisp; keep warm. Cut grilled pineapple into ½-inch cubes. Combine pineapple, onion, cilantro, lime juice, jalapeño pepper, garlic, salt and black pepper in medium bowl. Break tuna into bite-size chunks. Spoon pineapple salsa down center of each tortilla; top with tuna. Roll to enclose. Serve immediately. *Makes 4 servings*

Nutrients per Serving (2 tacos): Calories: 438, protein: 44 g, fat: 10 g, carbohydrate: 44, sodium: 296 mg, cholesterol: 64 mg

Herbed Butter Chicken

A mixture of fresh herbs, garlic and lemon peel tucked under the skin before grilling adds a flavor punch to chicken.

3 tablespoons minced fresh
    basil
2 teaspoons minced fresh
    oregano
2 teaspoons minced fresh
    rosemary
3 tablespoons minced shallots
    or green onion
2 tablespoons butter, softened
3 cloves garlic, minced

2 teaspoons grated lemon peel
½ teaspoon salt
¼ teaspoon black pepper
4 chicken legs with thighs *or*
    1 whole chicken (about
    3½ pounds), quartered
1 tablespoon olive oil
    Fresh oregano sprigs
    Lemon peel strips

Combine herbs, shallots, butter, garlic, lemon peel, salt and pepper in medium bowl. Loosen chicken skin by gently pushing fingers between the skin and chicken, keeping skin intact. Gently rub herb mixture under skin of chicken, forcing it into the leg section; secure skin with wooden picks. (Soak wooden picks in hot water 15 minutes to prevent burning.) Cover and refrigerate chicken at least ½ hour. Brush chicken with oil. Arrange medium Kingsford briquets on each side of rectangular metal or foil drip pan. Grill chicken, skin side down, in center of grid on covered grill 20 minutes. Turn chicken and cook 20 to 25 minutes or until juices run clear. Garnish with oregano sprigs and lemon strips.   *Makes 4 servings*

Nutrients per Serving: Calories: 347, protein: 30 g, fat: 24 g, carbohydrate: 2 g, sodium: 450 mg, cholesterol: 119 mg

Herbed Butter Chicken

Pork Tenderloin with Grilled Apple Cream Sauce

This delicate, lean pork tenderloin should be cooked just until it is barely pink in the center. Overcooking will cause pork to become dry.

1 can (6 ounces) frozen apple
  juice concentrate, thawed
  and divided (¾ cup)
½ cup Calvados or brandy,
  divided
2 tablespoons Dijon mustard
1 tablespoon olive oil
3 cloves garlic, minced
1¼ teaspoons salt, divided

¼ teaspoon black pepper
1½ pounds pork tenderloin
2 green or red apples, cored
1 tablespoon butter
½ large red onion, cut into
  thin slivers
½ cup heavy cream
  Fresh thyme sprigs

Reserve 2 tablespoons juice concentrate. Combine remaining juice concentrate, ¼ cup Calvados, mustard, oil, garlic, 1 teaspoon salt and pepper in glass dish. Add pork; turn to coat. Cover and refrigerate 2 hours, turning pork occasionally. Cut apples crosswise into ⅜-inch rings. Remove pork from marinade; discard marinade. Grill pork on covered grill over medium Kingsford briquets about 20 minutes, turning 3 times, until meat thermometer inserted in thickest part registers 155°F. Grill apples about 4 minutes per side until tender; cut rings into quarters. Melt butter in large skillet over medium heat. Add onion; cook and stir until soft. Stir in apples, remaining ¼ cup Calvados, ¼ teaspoon salt and reserved 2 tablespoons apple juice. Add cream; heat through. Cut pork crosswise into ½-inch slices; spoon sauce over pork. Garnish with fresh thyme.

Makes 4 servings

Nutrients per Serving: Calories: 462, protein: 40 g, fat: 21 g, carbohydrate: 19 g, sodium: 279 mg, cholesterol: 174 mg

Pork Tenderloin with
Grilled Apple Cream Sauce

Beef Direct Grilling Chart

Beef Cut (cooked yield per pound)	Thickness/ Weight	Approximate Cooking Time (uncovered over medium coals; medium-rare to medium doneness)
Tenderloin Steak Yields 4 (3-ounce) servings of cooked, trimmed beef per pound.	1 inch 1½ inches	13 to 15 minutes 14 to 16 minutes (covered)
Top Round Steak Yields 4 (3-ounce) servings of cooked, trimmed beef per pound.	¾ inch 1 inch 1½ inches	8 to 9 minutes* 16 to 18 minutes* 25 to 28 minutes* (covered)
Ground Beef Patties Yields 4 (3-ounce) servings of cooked beef per pound.**	½ × 4 inches	14 to 16 minutes
Boneless Top Loin Steak Yields 3¾ (3-ounce) servings of cooked, trimmed beef per pound.	¾ inch 1 inch	10 to 12 minutes 15 to 18 minutes
Boneless Top Sirloin Steak Yields 3½ (3-ounce) servings of cooked, trimmed beef per pound.	¾ inch 1 inch 1½ inches 2 inches	13 to 16 minutes 17 to 21 minutes 22 to 26 minutes (covered) 28 to 33 minutes (covered)
Chuck Shoulder Steak Yields 3½ (3-ounce) servings of cooked, trimmed beef per pound.	¾ inch 1 inch	14 to 17 minutes 16 to 20 minutes
Chuck Top Blade Steak Yields 3 (3-ounce) servings of cooked, trimmed beef per pound.	1 inch	18 to 22 minutes
Flank Steak Yields 4 (3-ounce) servings of cooked, trimmed beef per pound.	1½ to 2 pounds	17 to 21 minutes
Porterhouse/T-Bone Steak Yields 2½ (3-ounce) servings of cooked, trimmed beef per pound.	¾ inch 1 inch	10 to 12 minutes 14 to 16 minutes
Ribeye Steak Yields 3 (3-ounce) servings of cooked, trimmed beef per pound.	¾ inch 1 inch 1½ inches	6 to 8 minutes 11 to 14 minutes 17 to 22 minutes (covered)

Note: All cook times are based on beef removed directly from the refrigerator.

*Cook top round steak to medium-rare (145°F) doneness only.
**USDA recommends cooking ground beef patties to medium (160°F) doneness.

Chart courtesy of National Cattlemen's Beef Association.

Grilled Caribbean Steaks

Rubbing a dry marinade on meat results in a more intense flavor than a liquid marinade. For best flavor in this recipe, rub the steaks with the herb and spice mixture two or three days before cooking.

6 tablespoons brown sugar
2½ tablespoons paprika
2 tablespoons granulated
   sugar
1 tablespoon kosher salt
1 tablespoon chili powder
1¼ teaspoons granulated garlic
   or garlic powder
1¼ teaspoons dried oregano
   leaves

1¼ teaspoons dried basil leaves
¾ teaspoon dried thyme leaves
¾ teaspoon celery seed
¼ teaspoon cayenne pepper
2 lean beef T-bone steaks
   (12 to 16 ounces each),
   1 inch thick

To prepare spice mix, combine all ingredients except steak in small bowl; mix well. Measure out ¼ cup spice mix, reserving remaining for other uses.* Rub steaks with ¼ cup spice mix, using 1 tablespoon per side. Refrigerate steaks, covered, overnight or up to 3 days. Grill steaks on covered grill over medium Kingsford briquets 12 to 14 minutes for medium-rare or to desired doneness, turning once.

Makes 4 to 6 servings

*Recipe for spice mix makes 1¼ cups. Store leftover spice mix in covered container in cool, dry place. Use with beef, pork or chicken.

Nutrients per Serving (⅙ of recipe): Calories: 205, protein: 25 g, fat: 9 g, carbohydrate: 3 g, sodium: 297 mg, cholesterol: 72 mg

Thai Pork Salad

This salad is perfect for a quick dinner if the pork chops
are grilled when preparing Garlic-Pepper Skewered Pork (page 18);
otherwise grill boneless pork chops.

8 cups lightly packed
    shredded cabbage or
    packaged coleslaw mix
1 cup lightly packed cilantro
    leaves, coarsely chopped
30 large mint leaves, coarsely
    chopped
6 grilled pork loin chops
    (from Garlic-Pepper
    Skewered Pork, page 28)
    or 6 grilled ½-inch-thick
    boneless pork chops
2 tablespoons vegetable oil

½ large red onion, cut into
    thin slivers
½ cup lightly salted roasted
    cashews or peanuts
½ teaspoon salt
¼ to ½ teaspoon cayenne
    pepper
⅓ cup lime juice
1 tablespoon sugar
    Lime wedges
    Red onion strips
    Cilantro sprigs

Combine cabbage, cilantro and mint in large bowl; set aside. Cut pork
chops into ¼-inch-thick strips. Heat oil in large skillet over medium-high
heat. Add pork, onion, nuts, salt and cayenne pepper. Cook and stir
2 minutes; remove from heat. Stir in lime juice and sugar. Spoon pork
mixture over cabbage; toss well to coat. Garnish with lime wedges, onion
strips and cilantro.

*Makes 5 main-dish servings
or 8 to 10 side-dish servings*

Nutrients per Serving (1 main-dish serving): Calories: 281, protein: 18 g, fat: 15 g,
carbohydrate: 21 g, sodium: 496 mg, cholesterol: 41 mg

Thai Pork Salad

Express

Rosemary Steak

The aromatic combination of rosemary, garlic and lemon peel evokes the sun-drenched cuisines of the Mediterranean region. For a special meal, serve Rosemary Steak with grilled potato slices or garlic mashed potatoes and drizzle with Balsamic-Mushroom Vinaigrette (page 39).

4 boneless top loin beef steaks or New York strip steaks (about 6 ounces each)
2 tablespoons minced fresh rosemary
2 cloves garlic, minced
1 tablespoon extra-virgin olive oil

1 teaspoon grated lemon peel
1 teaspoon coarsely ground black pepper
½ teaspoon salt
Fresh rosemary sprigs

Score steaks in diamond pattern on both sides. Combine minced rosemary, garlic, oil, lemon peel, pepper and salt in small bowl; rub mixture onto surface of meat. Cover and refrigerate at least 15 minutes. Grill steaks over medium-hot Kingsford briquets about 4 minutes per side until medium-rare or to desired doneness. Cut steaks diagonally into ½-inch-thick slices. Garnish with rosemary sprigs.   *Makes 4 servings*

Nutrients per Serving: Calories: 328, protein: 42 g, fat: 16 g, carbohydrate: 1 g, sodium: 392 mg, cholesterol: 110 mg

Turkey Teriyaki Udon

Udon and soba are Japanese-style noodles. Udon is made
from wheat and soba from buckwheat. They are available fresh and
dried in Asian markets and dried in some large supermarkets.
Linguine can be substituted.

Turkey Teriyaki with Grilled
Mushrooms (page 44)
12 ounces fresh udon or soba
noodles
3 cups water
1 can (14 ounces) chicken
broth
2 tablespoons sake or sherry
wine

1 tablespoon minced fresh
ginger
1 tablespoon soy sauce
2 teaspoons sugar
1½ cups chopped fresh or
frozen spinach, thawed
1 cup fresh bean sprouts
Carrot flowers

Prepare Turkey Teriyaki with Grilled Mushrooms. Cook noodles according
to package directions; drain and keep warm. Combine water, broth, sake,
ginger, soy sauce and sugar in 5-quart Dutch oven. Bring to a boil over
high heat. Reduce heat to medium-low and simmer 5 minutes. Stir in
spinach and bean sprouts; heat through. Place noodles in 4 large soup
bowls; spoon broth mixture over noodles. Slice turkey into bite-size
pieces; arrange turkey, mushrooms and green onions on noodles. Garnish
with carrot flowers. Serve immediately.   *Makes 4 servings*

Nutrients per Serving: Calories: 398, protein: 44 g, fat: 4 g, carbohydrate: 46 g,
sodium: 830 mg, cholesterol: 89 mg

Turkey Teriyaki Udon

Southwest Chicken

**Prepare a double recipe–the leftovers make
great beginnings for quick weekday meals.**

2 tablespoons olive oil
1 clove garlic, pressed
1 teaspoon chili powder
1 teaspoon ground cumin
1 teaspoon dried oregano
    leaves

½ teaspoon salt
1 pound skinless boneless
    chicken breast halves or
    thighs

Combine oil, garlic, chili powder, cumin, oregano and salt; brush over
both sides of chicken to coat. Grill chicken over medium-hot Kingsford
briquets 8 to 10 minutes or until chicken is no longer pink, turning once.
Serve immediately or use in Build a Burrito, Taco Salad or other favorite
recipes. *Makes 4 servings*

Note: Southwest Chicken can be grilled ahead and refrigerated for several
days or frozen for longer storage.

Build a Burrito: Top warm large flour tortillas with strips of Southwest
Chicken and your choice of drained canned black beans, cooked brown
or white rice, shredded cheese, salsa verde, shredded lettuce, sliced black
olives and chopped cilantro. Fold in sides and roll to enclose filling. Heat
in microwave oven at HIGH until heated through. (Or, wrap in foil and
heat in preheated 350°F oven.)

Taco Salad: For a quick one-dish meal, layer strips of Southwest Chicken
with tomato wedges, blue or traditional corn tortilla chips, sliced black
olives, shredded romaine or iceberg lettuce, shredded cheese and avocado
slices. Serve with salsa, sour cream, guacamole or a favorite dressing.

Nutrients per Serving (Southwest Chicken): Calories: 202, protein: 26 g, fat: 10 g,
carbohydrate: 1 g, sodium: 362 mg, cholesterol: 70 mg

Taco Salad

Peanut Pork Lo Mein

Lo mein, a popular Chinese dish, consists of
boiled noodles, pork or chicken and vegetables seasoned
with a flavorful sauce. This sensational version has the added
dimension of smoky grilled pork and vegetables.

½ recipe Peanut Pork
Tenderloin (page 47), hot
and sliced into bite-size
pieces *or* ¾ pound pork
tenderloin, grilled and
sliced into bite-size pieces
1 package (12 ounces) fresh
chow mein noodles or
linguine
1 red bell pepper, cut into thin
slivers
1 small red onion, cut into
thin slivers

1½ cups snow peas, cut in half
diagonally
2 cloves garlic, minced
8 teaspoons vegetable oil,
divided
Salt and freshly ground
black pepper
2 tablespoons rice vinegar
2 tablespoons oyster sauce
2 tablespoons soy sauce
1 tablespoon dark sesame oil
2 green onions, thinly sliced
on diagonal

Prepare Peanut Pork Tenderloin. Cook noodles according to package
directions; drain and place in large bowl. Meanwhile, place bell pepper,
onion, snow peas and garlic in center of 18×12-inch sheet of heavy-duty
foil; drizzle with 2 teaspoons vegetable oil and season to taste with salt
and black pepper. Bring edges of foil up to form shallow pan. Grill
vegetables in foil pan on covered grill over medium Kingsford briquets
about 10 minutes until vegetables are crisp-tender, stirring gently several
times. Whisk together vinegar, oyster sauce, soy sauce, sesame oil and
remaining 6 teaspoons vegetable oil; pour over noodles, tossing to coat.
Arrange noodle mixture on large platter. Top with pork and vegetables;
garnish with green onions. Serve immediately.   *Makes 4 servings*

Nutrients per Serving: Calories: 466, protein: 29 g, fat: 18 g, carbohydrate: 47 g,
sodium: 1002 mg, cholesterol: 62 mg

Minty Lemon Chicken Soup

2 grilled Lemon-Garlic
    Chicken breast halves
    (page 42) or 2 grilled
    chicken breast halves
6 cups chicken broth, divided

1 cup uncooked long-grain rice
¼ cup lemon juice
¼ cup chopped fresh mint
Salt and black pepper

Prepare Lemon-Garlic Chicken. Bring 2 cups of chicken broth to a boil in large saucepan. Add rice; reduce heat to low and cook, covered, 15 minutes or until liquid has been absorbed. Stir in remaining 4 cups broth and lemon juice. Bring to a boil over high heat. Cut chicken into thin strips. Stir in chicken and mint. Season to taste with salt and pepper.

Makes 4 servings (about 2 cups each)

Nutrients per Serving: Calories: 331, protein: 24 g, fat: 7 g, carbohydrate: 40 g, sodium: 1344 mg, cholesterol: 35 mg

Balsamic-Mushroom Vinaigrette

**Simmering mushrooms in balsamic vinegar
gives this vinaigrette a rich mushroom flavor,
which complements grilled beef, fish and poultry.**

5 tablespoons extra-virgin
    olive oil, divided
¼ pound mushrooms, finely
    chopped
¼ cup water

2 tablespoons balsamic
    vinegar
1 teaspoon Dijon mustard
¼ teaspoon salt
3 tablespoons lemon juice

Heat 1 tablespoon oil in medium skillet over medium-high heat. Add mushrooms; cook and stir about 7 minutes until brown. Combine water, vinegar, mustard and salt in small bowl; add to mushrooms in skillet. Simmer until liquid is reduced by half. Remove from heat; whisk in lemon juice and remaining 4 tablespoons oil. Drizzle over grilled meats, poultry or fish.

Makes ¾ cup

Nutrients per Serving (3 tablespoons): Calories: 108, protein: trace, fat: 11 g, carbohydrate: 2 g, sodium: 123 mg, cholesterol: 0 mg

Tuna Vera Cruz

For a head start on tomorrow's dinner, prepare
a double recipe of this zesty tuna dish. Serve half
tonight and refrigerate the remaining tuna to make
Tuna Tacos with Grilled Pineapple Salsa (page 23).

3 tablespoons tequila, rum or
  vodka
2 tablespoons lime juice
2 teaspoons grated lime peel
1 piece (1-inch cube) fresh
  ginger, minced
2 cloves garlic, minced
1 teaspoon salt
1 teaspoon sugar

½ teaspoon ground cumin
¼ teaspoon ground cinnamon
¼ teaspoon black pepper
1 tablespoon vegetable oil
1½ pounds fresh tuna, halibut,
  swordfish or shark steaks
Lemon and lime wedges
Fresh rosemary sprigs

Combine tequila, lime juice, lime peel, ginger, garlic, salt, sugar, cumin,
cinnamon and pepper in 2-quart glass dish; stir in oil. Add tuna; turn
to coat. Cover and refrigerate at least 30 minutes. Remove tuna from
marinade; discard marinade. Grill tuna over medium-hot Kingsford
briquets about 4 minutes per side until fish flakes easily when tested
with fork. Garnish with lemon wedges, lime wedges and rosemary sprigs.

Makes 4 servings

Nutrients per Serving: Calories: 249, protein: 40 g, fat: 9 g, carbohydrate: 0 g,
sodium: 66 mg, cholesterol: 65 mg

Tuna Vera Cruz

Lemon-Garlic Chicken

*Grill an extra pound of chicken breast halves to use
for another meal of Minty Lemon Chicken Soup (page 39)
or Pasta Express (page 46) later in the week.*

2 tablespoons olive oil
2 cloves garlic, pressed
1 teaspoon grated lemon peel
1 teaspoon lemon juice
¼ teaspoon salt

¼ teaspoon black pepper
4 skinless boneless chicken
   breast halves (about
   1 pound)

Combine oil, garlic, lemon peel, lemon juice, salt and pepper in small
bowl. Brush oil mixture over both sides of chicken to coat. Lightly oil grid
to prevent sticking. Grill chicken over medium Kingsford briquets 8 to
10 minutes or until chicken is no longer pink in center, turning once.

Makes 4 servings

Nutrients per Serving: Calories: 199, protein: 26 g, fat: 10 g, carbohydrate: 1 g,
sodium: 208 mg, cholesterol: 70 mg

 # Sure-Fire Dessert

Barbecue Banana Split: Cut firm, ripe banana
lengthwise to, but not through, bottom peel. Brush cut sides with
melted butter; sprinkle with a little brown sugar. Grill 6 to
8 minutes on covered grill over medium-hot Kingsford briquets until
banana is heated through but still firm (peel will turn dark). Place
unpeeled banana in serving dish; top with small scoops of ice cream.
Drizzle with chocolate or caramel sauce. Top with whipped cream,
nuts and a cherry.

Backyard S'Mores

2 milk chocolate bars
(1.55 ounces each),
cut in half

8 large marshmallows
4 whole graham crackers
(8 squares)

Place each chocolate bar half and 2 marshmallows between 2 graham cracker squares. Wrap in lightly greased foil. Place on grill over medium-low Kingsford briquets about 3 to 5 minutes or until chocolate and marshmallows are melted. (Time will vary depending upon how hot coals are and whether grill is open or covered.) *Makes 4 servings*

Nutrients per Serving: Calories: 224, protein: 3 g, fat: 8 g, carbohydrate: 37 g, sodium: 117 mg, cholesterol: 6 mg

Grilled Fish with Roasted Jalapeño Rub

(Recipe adapted from Chef Randall Warder, Mansion on Turtle Creek, Dallas, TX)

3 tablespoons chopped
cilantro
2 tablespoons lime juice
1 tablespoon minced garlic
1 tablespoon minced fresh
ginger

1 tablespoon minced roasted
jalapeño peppers*
1½ pounds firm white fish
fillets, such as orange
roughy or red snapper
Lime wedges

Combine cilantro, lime juice, garlic, ginger and pepper in small bowl. Lightly oil grid to prevent sticking. Grill fish on covered grill over hot Kingsford briquets 5 minutes. Turn; spread cilantro mixture on fish. Grill 3 to 5 minutes longer or until fish flakes easily when tested with fork. Serve with lime wedges. *Makes 4 servings*

To roast peppers, place them on uncovered grill over hot coals. Grill until blistered, turning frequently. Remove from grill and place in large resealable plastic food storage bag for 15 minutes. Remove skins. Seed peppers, if desired, and cut into thin slices.

Nutrients per Serving: Calories: 236, protein: 33 g, fat: 10 g, carbohydrate: 2 g, sodium: 88 mg, cholesterol: 102 mg

Turkey Teriyaki with Grilled Mushrooms

Serve this dish right from the grill or use it to prepare Turkey Teriyaki Udon (page 34).

1¼ pounds turkey breast slices, tenderloins or medallions
¼ cup sake or sherry wine
¼ cup soy sauce
3 tablespoons granulated sugar, brown sugar or honey

1 piece (1-inch cube) fresh ginger, minced
3 cloves garlic, minced
1 tablespoon vegetable oil
½ pound mushrooms
4 green onions, cut into 2-inch pieces

Cut turkey into long 2-inch-wide strips.* Combine sake, soy sauce, sugar, ginger, garlic and oil in 2-quart glass dish. Add turkey; turn to coat. Cover and refrigerate 15 minutes or overnight. Remove turkey from marinade; discard marinade. Thread turkey onto metal or wooden skewers, alternating with mushrooms and green onions. (Soak wooden skewers in hot water 30 minutes to prevent burning.) Grill on covered grill over medium-hot Kingsford briquets about 3 minutes per side until turkey is cooked through.   *Makes 4 servings*

Do not cut tenderloins or medallions.

Nutrients per Serving: Calories: 173, protein: 34 g, fat: 2 g, carbohydrate: 5 g, sodium: 160 mg, cholesterol: 89 mg

Turkey Teriyaki with
Grilled Mushrooms

Pasta Express

Serve with a deli salad and hot crusty bread for a quick dinner.

2 grilled Lemon-Garlic Chicken breast halves (page 42) or 2 plain grilled chicken breast halves
1 package (9 ounces) lemon-pepper or plain linguine
¼ cup olive oil
½ medium yellow onion, sliced
3 cloves garlic, minced
1 cup grilled red or yellow bell pepper strips
¼ cup chopped fresh basil or parsley
1 cup freshly grated Parmesan cheese
Salt and black pepper

Prepare Lemon-Garlic Chicken; cut into thin slices. Cook linguine according to package directions until al dente; drain. Place in large bowl; keep warm. Heat oil in large skillet over medium heat. Add onion and garlic; cook and stir onion until crisp-tender. Add chicken, onion mixture, bell pepper, basil and cheese to linguine; season to taste with salt and black pepper. Toss until well mixed. *Makes 3 to 4 servings*

Nutrients per Serving (¼ of recipe): Calories: 564, protein: 30 g, fat: 26 g, carbohydrate: 53 g, sodium: 556 mg, cholesterol: 51 mg

 # Sure-Fire Dessert

Grilled Pineapple: Peel, core and cut pineapple into ¾-inch-thick rings or thin wedges. Brush generously with dark rum; sprinkle with brown sugar. Lightly oil grid to prevent sticking. Grill 8 to 10 minutes over medium-hot Kingsford briquets until warm and golden brown, turning once. Top each ring with 1 scoop of ice cream, frozen yogurt or sorbet and a sprinkling of toasted coconut.

Peanut Pork Tenderloin

**This Asian-inspired dish has flavors reminiscent
of Thai peanut sauce. Serve it with steamed rice and
grilled asparagus for a quick and easy meal.**

⅓ cup chunky unsweetened
    peanut butter
⅓ cup regular or light canned
    coconut milk
¼ cup lemon juice or dry white
    wine
3 tablespoons soy sauce
3 cloves garlic, minced

2 tablespoons sugar
1 piece (1-inch cube) fresh
    ginger, minced
½ teaspoon salt
¼ to ½ teaspoon cayenne
    pepper
¼ teaspoon ground cinnamon
1½ pounds pork tenderloin

Combine peanut butter, coconut milk, lemon juice, soy sauce, garlic, sugar,
ginger, salt, cayenne pepper and cinnamon in 2-quart glass dish until
blended. Add pork; turn to coat. Cover and refrigerate at least 30 minutes
or overnight. Remove pork from marinade; discard marinade. Grill pork
on covered grill over medium Kingsford briquets about 20 minutes until
just barely pink in center, turning 4 times. Cut crosswise into ½-inch
slices. Serve immediately. *Makes 4 to 6 servings*

Nutrients per Serving (⅙ of recipe): Calories: 248, protein: 39 g, fat: 8 g, carbohydrate: 2 g,
sodium: 217 mg, cholesterol: 125 mg

Vegetables, Salads & More

Sausage & Wilted Spinach Salad

¼ cup sherry vinegar or white
    wine vinegar
1 teaspoon whole mustard
    seeds, crushed
½ teaspoon salt
¼ teaspoon black pepper
2 ears corn, husked
1 large red onion, cut into
    ¾-inch-thick slices
4 tablespoons extra-virgin
    olive oil, divided

12 ounces smoked turkey,
    chicken or pork sausage
    links, such as Polish,
    Andouille or New Mexico
    style, cut in half
    lengthwise
2 cloves garlic, minced
10 cups lightly packed spinach
    leaves, torn
1 large avocado, peeled and
    cubed

Combine vinegar, mustard seeds, salt and pepper; set dressing aside. Brush corn and onion with 1 tablespoon oil. Insert wooden picks into onion slices from edges to prevent separating into rings. (Soak wooden picks in hot water 15 minutes to prevent burning.) Grill sausage, corn and onion over medium Kingsford briquets 6 to 10 minutes until vegetables are crisp-tender and sausage is hot, turning several times. Cut corn kernels from cobs; chop onion and slice sausage. Heat remaining 3 tablespoons oil in small skillet over medium heat. Add garlic; cook and stir 1 minute. Toss spinach, avocado, sausage, corn, onion and dressing in large bowl. Drizzle hot oil over salad; toss and serve immediately. *Makes 4 servings*

Nutrients per Serving: Calories: 477, protein: 16 g, fat: 37 g, carbohydrate: 26 g, sodium: 939 mg, cholesterol: 33 mg

Grilled Vegetable & Orzo Salad with Citrus Vinaigrette

½ cup thinly sliced shallots or green onions

⅓ cup white wine vinegar

¼ cup orange juice

2 tablespoons lemon juice

2 tablespoons extra-virgin olive oil

1½ teaspoons grated orange peel

1½ teaspoons grated lemon peel

1½ teaspoons salt

¼ teaspoon black pepper

10 large mushrooms, cut in half

1 package (10 ounces) frozen artichoke hearts, thawed

12 ounces orzo pasta, cooked, rinsed and drained

2 red or green bell peppers, cut in half, stemmed and seeded

12 large fresh basil leaves, minced (optional)

Orange peel strips

Combine shallots, vinegar, juices, oil, peels, salt and black pepper in large bowl; whisk until blended. Add mushrooms and artichokes; let stand 30 minutes. Thread artichokes and mushrooms onto wooden skewers; reserve vinaigrette. (Soak wooden skewers in hot water 30 minutes to prevent burning.) Add orzo to reserved dressing; toss to coat. Grill artichokes and mushrooms on covered grill over medium-hot Kingsford briquets 3 to 5 minutes per side. Grill bell peppers, skin sides down, over medium-hot briquets about 8 minutes until skins on all sides are charred. Place peppers in large resealable plastic food storage bag or paper bag; seal. Let stand 5 minutes; remove skin. Slice mushrooms and chop peppers; add to pasta with artichokes and basil, tossing until coated. Serve at room temperature. Garnish with orange peel strips.

Makes 8 side-dish servings (about 1 cup each)

Note: To make an entrée that serves four, add 1 can (15 ounces) rinsed and drained black beans *or* 2 cups cubed grilled chicken or sliced grilled sausage.

Nutrients per Serving: Calories: 209, protein: 7 g, fat: 13 g, carbohydrate: 16 g, sodium: 234 mg, cholesterol: 18 mg

Grilled Vegetable & Orzo Salad with Citrus Vinaigrette

Grilled Fresh Fruit

Fruit becomes slightly caramelized and picks up a
pleasant smoky flavor when cooked over smoldering coals.
Grilled fruit is a wonderful accompaniment to fish, poultry
and meat or a delicious topping for ice cream.

Fruit	Preparation for Grilling
Apples	cored and cut into ⅜-inch-thick rings
Apricots	cut in half and pitted
Cherries	pitted, if desired
Figs	whole or cut in half
Peaches and nectarines	peeled, if desired, pitted and sliced
Pears	cored and cut into ⅜-inch-thick rings
Pineapple	peeled, cored and cut into wedges or ½-inch-thick rings
Strawberries	large whole

Preparation: Brush fruit with melted butter or oil. Grill over medium-hot
Kingsford briquets 1 to 2 minutes per side or until lightly browned and
almost tender.

For a side dish: Place 2 cups grilled fruit slices or chunks in medium
bowl. Sprinkle with 2 tablespoons rice vinegar, 1 tablespoon olive oil and
2 teaspoons sugar; toss gently. *Makes 4 servings.*

For a dessert: Place 2 cups bite-size grilled fruit in a large bowl. Drizzle
with 1 to 2 tablespoons melted butter; toss gently. Sprinkle with
2 tablespoons sugar and drizzle with 4 tablespoons orange-flavored
liqueur. Serve over plain low-fat yogurt, vanilla ice cream or crème fraîche.
Makes 4 servings.

Grilled Banana Squash with Rum & Brown Sugar

Micro-grilling cuts grilling time in half. Partially cook the squash in a microwave oven and then finish cooking it on the grill.

2 pounds banana squash or
    butternut squash
2 tablespoons dark rum or
    apple juice

2 tablespoons melted butter
2 tablespoons brown sugar

Cut squash into 4 pieces; discard seeds. Place squash in microwavable baking dish. Cover with vented plastic wrap. Microwave at HIGH 5 to 7 minutes, turning once. Discard plastic wrap; pierce flesh of squash with fork at 1-inch intervals. Place squash in foil pan. Combine rum and butter; brush over squash. Sprinkle with sugar. Grill squash on covered grill over medium Kingsford briquets 20 to 30 minutes until squash is tender. *Makes 4 servings*

Nutrients per Serving: Calories: 170, protein: 2 g, fat: 6 g, carbohydrate: 31 g, sodium: 69 mg, cholesterol: 16 mg

Mediterranean Grilled Vegetables

4 medium red or Yukon gold
   potatoes, cooked
3 tablespoons orange juice
2 tablespoons balsamic
   vinegar
1 clove garlic, minced
½ teaspoon salt
¼ teaspoon black pepper
⅓ cup plus 3 tablespoons olive
   oil, divided
8 thin slices (4×2 inches)
   prosciutto or ham
   (optional)
3 ounces soft goat cheese, cut
   into 8 pieces (optional)

8 asparagus spears
2 red or yellow bell peppers,
   cut in half, stemmed and
   seeded
2 zucchini, cut lengthwise
   into ¼-inch slices
2 Japanese eggplants, cut
   lengthwise into
   ¼-inch slices
1 fennel bulb, cut in half
8 large mushrooms
2 poblano or green bell
   peppers, cut in half,
   stemmed and seeded

Cut potatoes into thick slices. Combine juice, vinegar, garlic, salt and black pepper in small bowl; whisk in ⅓ cup oil. Set aside. Wrap each slice prosciutto around 1 piece cheese and 1 asparagus spear. Thread cheese bundles onto wooden skewers, piercing asparagus and securing cheese with wooden picks, if necessary. (Soak wooden skewers and picks in hot water 30 minutes to prevent burning.) Brush bundles with 3 tablespoons remaining oil.

Grill bell peppers, skin sides down, over medium Kingsford briquets 8 minutes until skins are charred. Place in large resealable plastic food storage bag; seal. Let stand 5 minutes; remove skin. Grill remaining vegetables on covered grill over medium briquets 2 to 5 minutes per side until tender. Grill cheese bundles over medium briquets until lightly browned. Arrange vegetables and cheese bundles in 13×9-inch glass dish; drizzle with dressing, turning to coat. Let stand 15 minutes.

Makes 6 to 8 servings

Nutrients per Serving (⅛ of recipe): Calories: 168, protein: 5 g, fat: 7 g, carbohydrate: 26 g, sodium: 27 mg, cholesterol: 0 mg

Mediterranean Grilled Vegetables

Grilled Vegetables

Vegetable	Preparation for Grilling	Grilling Time
Beans, green	whole	5 minutes
Bell peppers or chili peppers	whole or cut in half, stemmed and seeded	10 to 20 minutes
Corn on cob	remove silk; soak unhusked corn in cold water 30 minutes	20 to 30 minutes
Eggplant, Japanese, Chinese and Italian	cut lengthwise into halves	20 minutes
Eggplant, traditional Western	cut into 1-inch-thick rounds	20 minutes
Leeks	whole, trim ends and discard tough outer layers	15 to 20 minutes
Mushrooms	stems removed	10 minutes
Onions, dry (yellow, white or red)	peel and cut into halves, wedges or rounds (To prevent separating, insert wooden picks into onions.*)	20 to 30 minutes
Onions, green	whole; roots and tops trimmed off	5 minutes
Potatoes	cut into ½-inch-thick rounds	10 to 12 minutes
Squash, summer	cut into halves or thick slices	5 to 10 minutes
Tomatoes	cut into halves or thick slices	5 to 10 minutes

Preparation: Brush vegetables lightly with vegetable oil. Season with chopped fresh or dried herbs, if desired. Thread small vegetables and pieces onto metal or wooden skewers* or place in grill basket; place large vegetables on grid. Grill vegetables over medium Kingsford briquets or around edges of hot briquets until tender, turning occasionally.

Soak wooden picks in hot water 15 minutes and wooden skewers 30 minutes to prevent burning.

Risotto with Grilled Vegetables

Grilled vegetables add a flavorful touch to a creamy risotto.

1 medium yellow onion, cut into ½-inch slices
1 zucchini, cut lengthwise into halves
Olive oil
1 *each* small red and yellow bell peppers
1 tablespoon butter
1 cup arborio rice

3 to 3½ cups canned chicken broth, divided
½ cup dry sherry
⅔ cup freshly grated Parmesan cheese
Black pepper
¼ cup toasted pine nuts
Chopped parsley

Insert wooden picks into onion slices from edges to prevent separating into rings. (Soak wooden picks in hot water 15 minutes to prevent burning.) Brush onion and zucchini lightly with oil. Grill onion, zucchini and bell peppers on covered grill over medium Kingsford briquets 5 to 10 minutes for zucchini and 20 to 30 minutes for peppers and onion or until crisp-tender. Cut vegetables into chunks. Heat butter and 1 tablespoon oil in 3-quart saucepan over medium heat. Add rice; cook and stir 3 to 4 minutes or until opaque. Add ¼ cup broth and sherry; cook 3 to 5 minutes over medium-low heat until almost all liquid is absorbed, stirring constantly. Continue adding broth in about ¾-cup increments, cooking and stirring after each addition until broth is absorbed and rice is tender and creamy. Stir in Parmesan cheese with last addition of broth. Season to taste with black pepper; stir in pine nuts and grilled vegetables, reserving a few for garnish. Spoon risotto into serving dish; top with reserved vegetables and parsley. *Makes 6 to 8 servings*

Nutrients per Serving (⅛ of recipe): Calories: 233, protein: 8 g, fat: 12 g, carbohydrate: 25 g, sodium: 440 mg, cholesterol: 9 mg

Fresh Grilled Corn Soup

Grilled Corn (recipe follows)
Grilled Onion (recipe
  follows)
2 medium potatoes, peeled
  and cubed
1 can (49½ ounces) chicken
  broth (about 6 cups)

½ teaspoon ground cumin
½ teaspoon chili powder
1½ cups heavy cream or
  half-and-half
Chopped fresh cilantro
½ teaspoon hot pepper sauce

Prepare Grilled Corn and Grilled Onion. Cut corn from cobs. Chop onion. Combine corn, onion, potatoes, broth, cumin and chili powder in Dutch oven. Bring to a boil. Reduce heat to medium-low; simmer about 30 minutes until potatoes are tender. Place in food processor in batches. Process until no large pieces remain, but mixture is not completely smooth. Return to Dutch oven; stir in cream, ⅓ cup cilantro and pepper sauce. Heat over low heat until warm. *Do not boil.* Ladle into bowls. Garnish with additional cilantro. *Makes 8 servings (1 cup each)*

Grilled Corn: Pull back husks from 4 ears of corn, leaving husks attached. Remove 1 strip of husk from inner portion of each ear and reserve; remove silk. Combine 1½ tablespoons melted butter, ½ teaspoon ground cumin, ¼ teaspoon chili powder and 1 teaspoon chopped fresh cilantro in small bowl; brush onto corn. Bring husks up each ear to cover corn; secure with reserved strips of husk. Grill on covered grill over medium Kingsford briquets 20 to 30 minutes or until tender, turning once or twice.

Grilled Onion: Cut 1 medium onion into ½-inch-thick rounds. Insert wooden picks into onion slices from edges to prevent separating into rings. (Soak wooden picks in hot water 15 minutes to prevent burning.) Brush onion slices with olive oil. Grill onion on covered grill over medium Kingsford briquets 20 to 30 minutes or until tender, turning once. Remove picks.

Nutrients per Serving: Calories: 199, protein: 7 g, fat: 10 g, carbohydrate: 22 g, sodium: 697 mg, cholesterol: 23 mg

Fresh Grilled Corn Soup

Grilled Garlic

Grilling lends a sweet, mellow flavor to garlic, making it an excellent addition to many dishes. Use it more generously than its fresh counterpart. Whenever you grill, place a head or two of garlic at the edge of the coals and grill alongside the main event.

1 or 2 heads garlic	**Olive oil**

Peel outermost papery skin from garlic heads. Brush heads with oil. Grill heads at edge of grid on covered grill over medium-hot Kingsford briquets 30 to 45 minutes or until cloves are soft and buttery. Remove from grill; cool slightly. Gently squeeze softened garlic head from root end so that cloves slip out of skins into small bowl. Use immediately or cover and refrigerate up to 1 week.

Serving Suggestions

• For a quick appetizer, spread cloves of Grilled Garlic over toasted bread slices, crackers or raw vegetable slices.

• Mash cloves of Grilled Garlic and add to baked potatoes, mashed potatoes, pasta dishes, soups, salad dressings and dips.

• Spread cloves of Grilled Garlic over bread slices for a flavorful, low-fat sandwich spread. Or, mash cloves and add to mayonnaise.

• Spread cloves of Grilled Garlic onto a pizza crust before adding toppings.

• To season steamed vegetables, mash cloves of Grilled Garlic and stir into melted or softened butter with chopped fresh herbs or spices.

Grilled Greek Vegetables

¼ cup olive oil	1 pound assorted fresh
1 tablespoon lemon juice	vegetables, such as
2 teaspoons pressed garlic	eggplant, bell peppers,
1 teaspoon dried oregano	summer squash,
leaves	mushrooms and onions

Combine oil, lemon juice, garlic and oregano in large bowl. Slice eggplant into ½-inch-thick rounds.* Cut small squash lengthwise into halves; cut large squash into ½-inch-thick pieces. Cut bell peppers into large chunks. Cut onions into wedges or thick slices. Toss vegetables with oil mixture to coat. Place vegetables in single layer on grid; reserve remaining oil mixture. Grill on covered grill over medium Kingsford briquets 10 to 20 minutes or until tender, turning once and basting with remaining oil mixture. *Makes 4 servings*

If desired, eggplant slices can be salted on both sides and placed in single layer on paper towels. Let stand 30 minutes; blot dry with paper towels.

Nutrients per Serving: Calories: 155, protein: 2 g, fat: 14 g, carbohydrate: 8 g, sodium: 4 mg, cholesterol: 0 mg

Stuffed Portobello Mushrooms

A dense, meaty texture makes portobello mushrooms ideal for stuffing and grilling. Serve them as an hors d'oeuvre or first course.

4 portobello mushrooms
   (4 ounces each)
¼ cup olive oil
2 cloves garlic, pressed
6 ounces crumbled goat
   cheese

2 ounces prosciutto or thinly
   sliced ham, chopped
¼ cup chopped fresh basil
Mixed salad greens

Remove stems and gently scrape gills from underside of mushrooms; discard stems and gills. Brush mushroom caps with combined oil and garlic. Combine cheese, prosciutto and basil in medium bowl. Grill mushrooms, top side up, on covered grill over medium Kingsford briquets 4 minutes. Turn mushrooms over; fill caps with cheese mixture, dividing equally. Cover and grill 3 to 4 minutes longer until cheese mixture is warm. Remove mushrooms from grill; cut into quarters. Serve on mixed greens. *Makes 4 servings*

Nutrients per Serving: Calories: 298, protein: 13 g, fat: 25 g, carbohydrate: 8 g, sodium: 353 mg, cholesterol: 28 mg

Salmon, Asparagus and Shiitake Salad

¼ cup cider vinegar
¼ cup extra-virgin olive oil
  Grated peel and juice of
    1 lemon
4 teaspoons Dijon mustard,
    divided
1 clove garlic, minced
¼ teaspoon salt
¼ teaspoon black pepper
2 teaspoons minced fresh
    tarragon *or* ¾ teaspoon
    dried tarragon leaves
1 pound small salmon fillets,
    skinned

1 medium red onion, thinly
    sliced
1 pound asparagus, ends
    trimmed
¼ pound shiitake mushrooms
    or button mushrooms
  Additional salt and black
    pepper
8 cups lightly packed torn
    romaine and red leaf
    lettuce

Combine vinegar, oil, juice, peel, 2 teaspoons mustard, garlic, ¼ teaspoon salt and ¼ teaspoon pepper in medium bowl; spoon 3 tablespoons dressing into 2-quart glass dish to use as marinade. Reserve remaining dressing. Add tarragon and 2 teaspoons remaining mustard to marinade in glass dish; blend well. Add salmon; turn to coat. Cover and refrigerate 1 hour. Transfer 3 tablespoons of reserved dressing to medium bowl; add onion, tossing to coat. Thread asparagus and mushrooms onto wooden skewers. (Soak skewers in hot water 30 minutes to prevent burning.)

Remove salmon from marinade; discard marinade. Season salmon to taste with additional salt and pepper. Lightly oil hot grid to prevent sticking. Grill salmon over medium-hot Kingsford briquets 2 to 4 minutes per side until fish flakes when tested with fork. Grill asparagus and mushrooms over medium-hot briquets 5 to 8 minutes until crisp-tender. Cut asparagus into 2-inch pieces and slice mushrooms; add to onion mixture. Let stand 10 minutes. Toss lettuce with onion mixture in large bowl; arrange lettuce on platter. Break salmon into 2-inch pieces; arrange salmon and vegetables over lettuce. Drizzle with remaining reserved dressing. Serve immediately.

Makes 4 main-dish servings

Nutrients per Serving: Calories: 282, protein: 24 g, fat: 16 g, carbohydrate: 13 g, sodium: 127 mg, cholesterol: 55 mg

Salmon, Asparagus and Shiitake Salad

Goat Cheese & Corn Chiles Rellenos

4 large plum tomatoes, seeded
   and diced
1 small red onion, diced and
   divided
3 tablespoons extra-virgin
   olive oil, divided
2 cloves garlic, minced and
   divided
1 teaspoon balsamic vinegar
¼ teaspoon salt
¼ teaspoon black pepper

6 poblano *or* 8 Anaheim
   peppers
2 ears corn, husked*
¾ cup crumbled goat or feta
   cheese
½ cup (2 ounces) shredded
   hot pepper Jack, Monterey
   Jack or sharp Cheddar
   cheese
½ cup minced fresh cilantro
   Fresh cilantro sprigs

Combine tomatoes, ½ onion, 2 tablespoons oil, 1 clove garlic, vinegar, salt and black pepper in medium bowl; let salsa stand 15 minutes. Remove stems from poblano peppers by cutting each pepper about ½ inch from stem; remove seeds. Grill peppers over medium-hot Kingsford briquets until skins are charred on all sides. Place peppers in large resealable plastic food storage bag; seal. Let stand 5 minutes; remove skin. Grill corn over medium-hot briquets 6 to 10 minutes or until tender, turning every minute; cut kernels from cob. Combine corn, cheeses, minced cilantro, remaining ½ onion and 1 clove garlic in medium bowl; mix well. Carefully fill each pepper with cheese mixture, making cut in side of pepper, if necessary. Secure opening with wooden pick. (Soak wooden picks in hot water 15 minutes to prevent burning.) Brush peppers with remaining 1 tablespoon oil; grill over medium briquets 1 minute per side until cheese melts. Serve with salsa. Garnish with cilantro sprigs.

Makes 6 servings

Substitute 1 can (17 ounces) corn, drained, or 1½ cups frozen corn, thawed, for fresh corn, if desired. Add to filling as directed above.

Nutrients per Serving: Calories: 209, protein: 7 g, fat: 13 g, carbohydrate: 16 g, sodium: 234 mg, cholesterol: 18 mg

Goat Cheese & Corn Chile Relleno

Pizzas, Sandwiches & More

Grilled Chile Chicken Quesadillas

2 tablespoons lime juice
3 cloves garlic, minced
1 tablespoon ground cumin
1 tablespoon chili powder
1 tablespoon vegetable oil
1 jalapeño pepper, minced
1 teaspoon salt
6 skinless boneless chicken
    thighs

3 poblano peppers, cut in half,
    stemmed, seeded
2 avocados, peeled and sliced
3 cups (12 ounces) shredded
    Monterey Jack cheese
12 (8-inch) flour tortillas
1½ cups fresh salsa
    Red chiles
    Fresh cilantro sprigs

Combine lime juice, garlic, cumin, chili powder, oil, jalapeño pepper and
salt in small bowl; coat chicken with paste. Cover and refrigerate chicken
at least 15 minutes. Grill chicken on covered grill over medium-hot
Kingsford briquets 4 minutes per side until no longer pink in center.
Grill poblano peppers, skin side down, 8 minutes until skins are charred.
Place peppers in large resealable plastic food storage bag; seal. Let stand
5 minutes; remove skin. Cut chicken and peppers into strips. Arrange
chicken, peppers, avocado and cheese on half of each tortilla. Drizzle with
2 tablespoons salsa. Fold other half of tortilla over filling. Grill quesadillas
on covered grill over medium briquets 30 seconds to 1 minute per side
until cheese is melted. Garnish with chiles and cilantro sprigs.

Makes 12 quesadillas

Nutrients per Serving (1 quesadilla): Calories: 363, protein: 18 g, fat: 18 g, carbohydrate: 26 g,
sodium: 695 mg, cholesterol: 58 mg

Grilled Chile Chicken Quesadillas

Magic Carpet Kabobs

Marinate chicken thighs overnight in a marinade reminiscent
of the exotic flavors of the cuisines of far-off lands.

1 cup orange juice	1 teaspoon red pepper flakes
½ cup bottled mango chutney, divided	¼ teaspoon salt
2 tablespoons lemon juice	4 skinless boneless chicken thighs, cut into chunks
1 tablespoon grated fresh ginger	1 medium yellow onion, cut into chunks
2 cloves garlic, pressed	4 whole pita bread rounds
2 teaspoons ground cumin	½ cup plain low-fat yogurt
1 teaspoon grated lemon peel	¾ cup chopped cucumber
1 teaspoon grated orange peel	Orange peel strips

Combine orange juice, ¼ cup chutney, lemon juice, ginger, garlic, cumin, grated peels, pepper and salt, blending well; reserve ¼ cup marinade for basting. Combine remaining marinade and chicken in large resealable plastic food storage bag. Seal bag; turn to coat evenly. Marinate in refrigerator overnight. Thread chicken alternately with onion onto 4 long wooden skewers, dividing equally. (Soak wooden skewers in hot water 30 minutes to prevent burning.) Lightly oil grid to prevent sticking. Grill kabobs over medium-hot Kingsford briquets 10 to 12 minutes until chicken is no longer pink, turning once and basting with reserved marinade. Grill pita breads 1 or 2 minutes until warm. Combine yogurt and remaining ¼ cup chutney. Spoon yogurt mixture down centers of pitas; top with cucumber, dividing equally. Top each with kabob; remove skewer. Garnish with orange peel strips. *Makes 4 servings*

Nutrients per Serving: Calories: 282, protein: 24 g, fat: 17 g, carbohydrate: 8 g, sodium: 676 mg, cholesterol: 70 mg

Magic Carpet Kabob

Pesto Chicken & Pepper Wraps

Purchased pesto sauce is the secret to these quick and delicious wraps.
It flavors the marinade and then it is spread on the tortillas.

⅔ cup refrigerated pesto sauce
    or frozen pesto sauce,
    thawed and divided
3 tablespoons red wine
    vinegar
¼ teaspoon salt
¼ teaspoon black pepper
1¼ pounds skinless boneless
    chicken thighs or breasts
2 red bell peppers, cut in half,
    stemmed and seeded

5 (8-inch) flour tortillas
5 thin slices (3-inch rounds)
    fresh-pack mozzarella
    cheese*
5 leaves Boston or red leaf
    lettuce
Orange slices
Red and green chiles
Fresh basil sprigs

Combine ¼ cup pesto, vinegar, salt and black pepper in medium bowl.
Add chicken; toss to coat. Cover and refrigerate at least 30 minutes.
Remove chicken from marinade; discard marinade. Grill chicken over
medium-hot Kingsford briquets about 4 minutes per side until chicken is
no longer pink in center, turning once. Grill bell peppers, skin sides down,
about 8 minutes until skin is charred. Place bell peppers in large resealable
plastic food storage bag; seal. Let stand 5 minutes; remove skin. Cut
chicken and bell peppers into thin strips. Spread about 1 tablespoon of
remaining pesto down center of each tortilla; top with chicken, bell
peppers, cheese and lettuce. Roll tortillas to enclose filling. Garnish with
orange slices, chiles and basil sprigs. *Makes 5 wraps*

Packaged sliced whole milk or part-skim mozzarella cheese can be substituted for fresh-pack mozzarella cheese.

Nutrients per Serving (1 wrap): Calories: 481, protein: 40 g, fat: 24 g, carbohydrate: 26 g,
sodium: 596 mg, cholesterol: 106 mg

Pesto Chicken & Pepper Wrap

Caramelized Onion & Eggplant Sandwiches

Eggplant and onion soak up the flavors of Southeast Asian cuisines in this vegetarian sandwich.

Grilled Garlic Aioli (recipe follows) or mayonnaise
½ cup packed brown sugar
½ cup water
½ cup soy sauce
2 tablespoons molasses
5 slices fresh ginger
¼ teaspoon ground coriander
Dash black pepper

1 large yellow onion
4 large eggplant slices, 1 inch thick
4 round buns, split
4 tomato slices
Mixed greens
Radishes
Carrot curls

Prepare Grilled Garlic Aioli; set aside. Combine sugar, water, soy sauce, molasses, ginger, coriander and pepper in small saucepan. Bring to boil, stirring constantly. Reduce heat; simmer marinade 5 minutes, stirring occasionally. Cool. Cut onion into ½-inch-thick slices. Insert wooden picks into onion slices from edges to prevent separating into rings. (Soak wooden picks in hot water 15 minutes to prevent burning.) Marinate eggplant and onion in marinade 10 to 15 minutes. Remove vegetables from marinade; reserve marinade. Lightly oil grid to prevent sticking. Grill vegetables on covered grill around edge of medium-hot Kingsford briquets about 20 minutes or until tender, turning once or twice and brushing with reserved marinade. Place buns on grill, cut sides down, until toasted. Serve eggplant and onion on grilled buns with tomato, greens and Grilled Garlic Aioli. Garnish with radishes and carrot curls.

Makes 4 sandwiches

Grilled Garlic Aioli: Prepare Grilled Garlic (page 60). Mash 8 cloves Grilled Garlic in small bowl. Add ¼ cup mayonnaise; mix until blended.

Nutrients per Serving: Calories: 334, protein: 7 g, fat: 15 g, carbohydrate: 46 g, sodium: 414 mg, cholesterol: 21 mg

Caramelized Onion & Eggplant Sandwich

Vietnamese Grilled Steak Wraps

Each bite teases the taste buds with the flavors of fresh mint, cilantro, tangy lemon and fiery chile sauce. Heavenly!

1 beef flank steak (about 1½ pounds)
Grated peel and juice of 2 lemons
6 tablespoons sugar, divided
2 tablespoons dark sesame oil
1¼ teaspoons salt, divided
½ teaspoon black pepper
¼ cup water
¼ cup rice vinegar
½ teaspoon crushed red pepper
6 (8-inch) flour tortillas
6 red leaf lettuce leaves
⅓ cup lightly packed fresh mint leaves
⅓ cup lightly packed fresh cilantro leaves
Star fruit slices
Red bell pepper strips
Orange peel strips

Cut beef across the grain into thin slices. Combine lemon peel, juice, 2 tablespoons sugar, sesame oil, 1 teaspoon salt and black pepper in medium bowl. Add beef; toss to coat. Cover and refrigerate at least 30 minutes. Combine water, vinegar, remaining 4 tablespoons sugar and ¼ teaspoon salt in small saucepan; bring to a boil. Boil 5 minutes without stirring until syrupy. Stir in crushed red pepper; set aside.

Remove beef from marinade; discard marinade. Thread beef onto metal or wooden skewers. (Soak wooden skewers in hot water 30 minutes to prevent burning.) Grill beef over medium-hot Kingsford briquets about 3 minutes per side until cooked through. Grill tortillas until hot. Place lettuce, beef, mint and cilantro on tortillas; drizzle with vinegar mixture. Roll tortillas to enclose filling. Garnish with star fruit, bell pepper and orange peel strips. *Makes 6 wraps*

Nutrients per Serving (1 wrap): Calories: 366, protein: 25 g, fat: 16 g, carbohydrate: 28 g, sodium: 340 mg, cholesterol: 61 mg

Vietnamese Grilled Steak Wrap

Grilled Garlic & Herb Pizzas

**Homemade Pizza Dough
(page 78)
8 cloves Grilled Garlic
(page 60)
1 medium yellow onion
Olive oil
1 medium red, yellow or
orange bell pepper**

**1 cup crumbled goat cheese
¼ cup chopped fresh herb
mixture (thyme, basil,
oregano and parsley)** *or*
**4 teaspoons dry herb
mixture
¼ cup grated Parmesan cheese**

Prepare Homemade Pizza Dough. While dough is rising, light Kingsford briquets in covered grill. Arrange medium-hot briquets on one side of the grill. Prepare Grilled Garlic. Lightly oil grid to prevent sticking. Cut onion into ½-inch-thick slices. Insert wooden picks into onion slices from edges to prevent separating into rings. (Soak wooden picks in hot water 15 minutes to prevent burning.) Brush onion lightly with oil. Place whole bell pepper and onion slices on grid around edge of briquets. Grill on covered grill 20 to 30 minutes until tender, turning once or twice. Remove picks from onion slices and separate into rings. Cut pepper in half and remove seeds; slice pepper halves into strips.

Roll or gently stretch each ball of dough into 7-inch round. Brush lightly with oil on both sides. Grill dough on grid directly above medium-hot Kingsford briquets 1 to 3 minutes or until dough starts to bubble and bottom is lightly browned. Turn; grill 3 to 5 minutes or until second side is lightly browned and dough is cooked through. Remove from grill. Spread 2 cloves Grilled Garlic onto each crust; top with onion, pepper, goat cheese, herbs and Parmesan cheese, dividing equally. Place pizzas around edge of coals; grill covered 5 minutes until bottom crust is crisp, cheese melts and toppings are heated through.

Makes 4 individual pizzas

Note: A 1-pound loaf of frozen bread dough, thawed, can be substituted for Homemade Pizza Dough. Or, substitute 4 pre-baked individual Italian bread shells, add toppings and warm on the grill.

continued on page 78

Grilled Garlic & Herb Pizzas

Grilled Garlic & Herb Pizzas, continued

Homemade Pizza Dough

2¾ cups all-purpose flour, divided

1 package quick-rising yeast

¾ teaspoon salt

1 cup water

1½ tablespoons vegetable oil

Combine 1½ cups flour, yeast and salt in food processor. Heat water and oil in small saucepan until 120° to 130°F. With food processor running, add water and oil to flour mixture; process 30 seconds. Add 1 cup flour; process until dough comes together to form ball. Knead on floured board 3 to 4 minutes or until smooth and satiny, kneading in as much of the remaining ¼ cup flour as needed to prevent dough from sticking. Place dough in oiled bowl, turning once. Cover with towel; let rise in warm place 30 minutes until doubled in bulk. Divide dough into 4 equal balls.

Nutrients per Serving (1 individual pizza): Calories: 533, protein: 19 g, fat: 21 g, carbohydrate: 68 g, sodium: 668 mg, cholesterol: 20 mg

Cajun Catfish Sandwiches

Make an extra batch of seasoning mix to keep on hand.

Aioli Tartar Sauce (page 79)

4½ teaspoons paprika

1 tablespoon dried oregano leaves

1½ teaspoons salt

¾ teaspoon granulated garlic

½ teaspoon white pepper

½ teaspoon black pepper

½ teaspoon cayenne pepper

4 small catfish fillets (1¼ pounds)

Lemon juice

4 sourdough rolls, split

4 cups finely shredded cabbage

Lemon wedges

Prepare Aioli Tartar Sauce; set aside. Combine paprika, oregano, salt, garlic and peppers until blended. Brush catfish with lemon juice; sprinkle evenly with seasoning mix to coat. Lightly oil grid to prevent sticking. Grill over medium-hot Kingsford briquets, allowing 10 minutes cooking time for each inch of thickness, turning once. Spread Aioli Tartar Sauce onto insides of rolls. Top each roll with catfish fillet and 1 cup cabbage. Serve with lemon wedges. *Makes 4 sandwiches*

Aioli Tartar Sauce: Prepare Grilled Garlic (page 60). Combine ½ cup mayonnaise, 12 mashed cloves Grilled Garlic, 2 teaspoons *each* lemon juice and chopped parsley, and 1 teaspoon chopped, drained capers; blend well.

Nutrients per Serving: Calories: 508, protein: 33 g, fat: 30 g, carbohydrate: 29 g, sodium: 1296 mg, cholesterol: 98 mg

Turkey Picatta on Grilled Rolls

¼ **cup lemon juice**
¼ **cup olive oil**
2 **tablespoons capers in liquid, chopped**
2 **cloves garlic, pressed**
   Black pepper
1 **pound turkey breast slices**
4 **soft French rolls, cut into halves**

4 **thin slices mozzarella or Swiss cheese (optional)**
   Lettuce (optional)
   Red bell pepper slivers (optional)
   Additional capers (optional)

Combine lemon juice, oil, 2 tablespoons capers with liquid, garlic and black pepper to taste in shallow glass dish or large resealable plastic food storage bag. Add turkey; turn to coat. Cover and marinate in refrigerator several hours or overnight. Remove turkey from marinade; discard marinade. Lightly oil grid to help prevent sticking. Grill turkey over medium-hot Kingsford briquets 2 minutes until turkey is no longer pink, turning once. Move cooked turkey slices to edge of grill to keep warm. Grill rolls, cut sides down, until toasted. Fill rolls with hot turkey slices, dividing equally. Add cheese, lettuce, bell pepper and additional capers, if desired. *Makes 4 servings*

Nutrients per Serving: Calories: 295, protein: 31 g, fat: 3 g, carbohydrate: 31 g, sodium: 374 mg, cholesterol: 73 mg

Barbecue Pizzas

Homemade Pizza Dough
(page 78)
1 medium yellow onion
Olive oil
½ cup plus 2 tablespoons
K.C. Masterpiece Original
Barbecue Sauce, divided

6 ounces thinly sliced grilled
pork or chicken
2 cups (8 ounces) shredded
smoked Gouda or
mozzarella cheese
¼ cup chopped fresh cilantro

Prepare Homemade Pizza Dough. While dough is rising, light Kingsford briquets in grill. Arrange medium-hot briquets on one side of grill. Lightly oil grid to prevent sticking. Slice onion into ½-inch-thick slices. Insert wooden picks into onion slices from edges to prevent separating into rings. (Soak wooden picks in hot water 15 minutes to prevent burning.) Brush onion lightly with oil. Place on grid around edge of briquets. Grill onion on covered grill 20 to 30 minutes or until tender. Brush with 2 tablespoons barbecue sauce during last 5 minutes of grilling. Remove picks and separate onion into rings; set aside.

Roll or gently stretch each ball of dough into 7-inch round. Brush lightly with oil on both sides. Grill dough on grid directly above medium-hot Kingsford briquets 1 to 3 minutes or until dough starts to bubble and bottom is lightly browned. Turn; grill 3 to 5 minutes or until second side is lightly browned and dough is cooked through. Remove from grill. Brush crusts with remaining ½ cup barbecue sauce; top with grilled pork, onion rings, cheese and cilantro, dividing equally. Place pizzas around edge of briquets; grill covered about 5 minutes until bottom crust is crisp, cheese melts and toppings are heated through.   *Makes 4 individual pizzas*

Note: A 1-pound loaf of frozen bread dough, thawed, can be substituted for Homemade Pizza Dough. Or, substitute pre-baked individual Italian bread shells. Add toppings and warm on grill.

Nutrients per Serving: Calories: 688, protein: 35 g, fat: 29 g, carbohydrate: 70 g, sodium: 1035 mg, cholesterol: 88 mg

SALADS, SIDES & MORE

CONTENTS

AMAZING APPETIZERS

Toasted Pesto Rounds

¼ **cup thinly sliced fresh basil or chopped fresh dill**
¼ **cup (1 ounce) grated Parmesan cheese**
1 **medium clove garlic, minced**
3 **tablespoons reduced-fat mayonnaise**
12 **French bread slices, about ¼ inch thick**
4 **teaspoons chopped tomato**
1 **green onion with top, sliced**
 Black pepper

1. Preheat broiler.

2. Combine basil, cheese, garlic and mayonnaise in small bowl; mix well.

3. Arrange bread slices in single layer on large nonstick baking sheet or broiler pan. Broil, 6 to 8 inches from heat, 30 to 45 seconds or until bread slices are lightly toasted.

4. Turn bread slices over; spread evenly with basil mixture. Broil 1 minute or until lightly browned. Top evenly with tomato and green onion. Season to taste with pepper. Transfer to serving plate. *Makes 12 servings*

Cherry Tomato Appetizers

1 pint cherry tomatoes
   Ice water
½ cup sliced green onions
¼ cup LAWRY'S® Lemon Pepper Marinade with Lemon Juice

In large pan of rapidly boiling water, carefully immerse tomatoes 15 seconds. Remove with slotted spoon and immediately submerge in ice water. Peel off and discard skins and stems. In large resealable plastic food storage bag, place tomatoes. Add green onions and Lemon Pepper Marinade; seal bag. Marinate in refrigerator at least 30 minutes.

Makes 4 servings

SERVING SUGGESTION: Serve as an appetizer with wooden picks or as a side dish.

Chili Garlic Prawns

2 tablespoons vegetable oil
1 pound prawns, peeled and deveined
3 tablespoons LEE KUM KEE® Chili Garlic Sauce
1 green onion, cut into slices

1. Heat oil in wok or skillet. Add prawns and stir-fry until just pink.

2. Add chili garlic sauce and stir-fry until prawns are completely cooked. Sprinkle with green onion and serve.

Makes 4 servings

Campbell's® Nacho Tacos

1 pound ground beef
1 medium onion, chopped (about ½ cup)
½ teaspoon chili powder
1 can (11 ounces) CAMPBELL'S® Condensed Fiesta Nacho
    Cheese Soup
8 taco shells
1 cup shredded lettuce
1 medium tomato, chopped (about 1 cup)

1. In medium skillet over medium-high heat, cook beef, onion and chili powder until beef is browned, stirring to separate meat. Pour off fat.

2. Add ½ *cup* soup and heat through.

3. In small saucepan over low heat, heat remaining soup until hot. Divide meat mixture among taco shells. Top with **1½ tablespoons** hot soup, lettuce and tomato.

Makes 8 tacos

Prep Time: 10 minutes
Cook Time: 10 minutes

Pace® Chili con Queso Bites

4 eggs
½ cup PACE® Picante Sauce _or_ Thick & Chunky Salsa
¼ cup all-purpose flour
2 teaspoons chili powder
1½ cups shredded Cheddar cheese (6 ounces)
1 green onion, chopped (about 2 tablespoons)

1. Preheat oven to 400°F. Grease 24 (3-inch) muffin-pan cups. Set aside.

2. In medium bowl mix eggs, picante sauce, flour and chili powder. Stir in cheese and onion.

3. Spoon about **_1 tablespoon_** cheese mixture into each cup. Bake 10 minutes or until golden brown. Serve warm or at room temperature with sour cream and additional picante sauce if desired. _Makes 24 appetizers_

T ip: Baked appetizers may be frozen. To reheat, bake frozen appetizers at 350°F. for 10 minutes or until hot.

Prep Time: 10 minutes
Cook Time: 10 minutes

V8® Bloody Mary Mocktail (page 88), and
Pace® Chili con Queso Bites

V8® Bloody Mary Mocktail

3 cups V8® 100% Vegetable Juice
1 teaspoon prepared horseradish
1 teaspoon Worcestershire sauce
½ teaspoon hot pepper sauce
Lemon slices for garnish

Mix vegetable juice, horseradish, Worcestershire and hot pepper sauce. Serve over ice. Garnish with lemon slices.

Makes 3 cups

HOT 'N' SPICY MOCKTAIL: Increase prepared horseradish to **1 tablespoon**.

Prep Time: 5 minutes

Garlic & Herb Dip

1 cup reduced-fat sour cream
¼ cup reduced-fat mayonnaise
2 tablespoons snipped green onion
1 clove garlic, minced
1 teaspoon dried basil leaves
½ teaspoon dried tarragon leaves
¼ teaspoon salt
¼ teaspoon black pepper
Assorted fresh vegetable dippers or pita chips

Combine all ingredients except dippers in medium bowl until blended. Cover; refrigerate several hours or overnight. Serve with dippers.

Makes about 1¼ cups

Lit'l Wiener Kabobs

30 HILLSHIRE FARM® Lit'l Smokies
 4 dill pickles, cut into ¾-inch pieces
 1 pint cherry tomatoes
 1 can (4 ounces) button mushrooms, drained
15 large pimiento-stuffed green olives
 1 green bell pepper, cut into ¾-inch squares
   Lemon Butter (recipe follows)

Preheat oven to 450°F.

Thread 2 Lit'l Smokies each onto 15 skewers, alternating with pickles, tomatoes, mushrooms, olives and pepper. Place skewers on rack in broiler pan. Prepare Lemon Butter; brush skewers with butter. Bake 4 to 6 minutes or until hot.

Makes 15 hors d'oeuvres

Lemon Butter

 2 tablespoons butter
 1 teaspoon lemon juice
   Dash hot pepper sauce

Combine all ingredients in small saucepan over medium-low heat; heat until butter is melted.

Makes about 2½ tablespoons

Tex-Mex Guacamole Platter

4 ripe avocados
¼ cup lime juice
3 large cloves garlic, crushed
2 tablespoons olive oil
½ teaspoon salt
¼ teaspoon black pepper
1 cup (4 ounces) shredded Colby-Jack cheese
1 cup seeded, diced plum tomatoes
⅓ cup sliced and pitted ripe olives
⅓ cup prepared salsa
1 tablespoon minced fresh cilantro
Tortilla chips

Cut avocados in half, remove pits and scoop out flesh into food processor. Add lime juice, garlic, olive oil, salt and pepper. Process until almost smooth.

Spread avocado mixture evenly on large dinner plate or serving platter, leaving a border around edge. Top with cheese, tomatoes, olives, salsa and cilantro. Serve with chips.

Makes 6 to 8 servings

Tex-Mex Guacamole Platter

Campbell's® Nachos Grande

**1 can (11 ounces) CAMPBELL'S® Condensed Fiesta Nacho
   Cheese Soup**
⅓ cup milk
1 pound ground beef
1 small onion, chopped (about ¼ cup)
5 cups tortilla chips (about 5 ounces)
1 medium tomato, chopped (about 1 cup)
1 jalapeño pepper, seeded and sliced (optional)

1. In small saucepan mix soup and milk. Set aside.

2. In medium skillet over medium-high heat, cook beef and onion until beef is browned, stirring to separate meat. Pour off fat. Add **½ cup** soup mixture. Reduce heat to low and heat through.

3. Over medium heat, heat remaining soup mixture, stirring often.

4. Arrange chips on large platter and top with meat mixture. Spoon soup mixture over meat. Top with tomato and pepper.

Makes 8 appetizer servings

Prep Time: 10 minutes
Cook Time: 10 minutes

*Top to bottom: Campbell's® Nachos Grande and
Campbell's® Nacho Tacos (page 85)*

SUPER SALADS

Mediterranean Greek Salad

½ cup olive oil
⅓ cup red wine vinegar
2 teaspoons chopped fresh oregano *or* ¾ teaspoon dried oregano
1 teaspoon LAWRY'S® Seasoned Salt
1 teaspoon LAWRY'S® Garlic Powder with Parsley
3 medium cucumbers, peeled and chopped
3 to 4 medium tomatoes, seeded and coarsely chopped
1 medium onion, thinly sliced and separated into rings
1 can (6 ounces) Greek or ripe olives, drained, pitted
1 cup (4 ounces) crumbled feta cheese

In container with stopper or lid, combine oil, vinegar, oregano and seasonings. Cover; shake well. Set dressing aside. In medium bowl, combine cucumbers, tomatoes, onion, olives and cheese; mix lightly. Shake dressing. Add to salad; toss lightly to coat. Refrigerate 30 minutes.   *Makes 8 servings*

SERVING SUGGESTION: Serve with heated pita bread and spread with herb-flavored butter.

HINT: Substitute a Lawry's® classic dressing such as Caesar or Red Wine Vinaigrette for first 5 ingredients.

Spinach, Bacon and Mushroom Salad

1 large bunch (12 ounces) fresh spinach leaves, washed,
    drained and torn
¾ cup sliced fresh mushrooms
4 slices bacon, cooked and crumbled
¾ cup croutons
4 hard-cooked eggs, finely chopped
    Black pepper, to taste
¾ cup prepared HIDDEN VALLEY® Original Ranch® Salad
    Dressing & Recipe Mix

In medium salad bowl, combine spinach, mushrooms and
bacon; toss. Top with croutons and eggs; season with pepper.
Pour salad dressing over all. *Makes 6 servings*

Elegant Spring Salad

DRESSING
¼ cup seasoned rice vinegar
2 tablespoons WESSON® Oil
1 tablespoon LA CHOY® Soy Sauce
1 tablespoon sugar
1 teaspoon minced gingerroot
¼ teaspoon *each:* pepper and Oriental sesame oil

SALAD
4 cups torn spinach leaves
2 cups chopped cooked chicken
2 (11-ounce) cans mandarin oranges, drained
1 (14-ounce) can LA CHOY® Bean Sprouts, drained
2 tablespoons sliced green onions
1 (5-ounce) can LA CHOY® Chow Mein Noodles

In small bowl, whisk together dressing ingredients; set aside. In large bowl, combine all salad ingredients except noodles. Add dressing; toss gently to coat. Cover; chill 1 hour. Top with noodles just before serving. *Makes 5 servings*

Asian Slaw

½ **small head napa cabbage, shredded (about 4 cups)***
3 **carrots, shredded**
2 **red or yellow bell peppers, seeded and cut into very thin strips**
¼ **pound snow peas, trimmed and cut into thin strips**
⅓ **cup peanut oil**
¼ **cup rice vinegar**
3 **tablespoons FRENCH'S® Worcestershire Sauce**
1 **tablespoon Oriental sesame oil**
1 **tablespoon honey**
2 **cloves garlic, minced**

*You may substitute 4 cups shredded green cabbage for the napa cabbage.

Place vegetables in large bowl. Whisk together peanut oil, vinegar, Worcestershire, sesame oil, honey and garlic in small bowl until well blended. Pour dressing over vegetables; toss well to coat evenly. Cover and refrigerate 1 hour before serving. *Makes 6 side-dish servings*

Prep Time: 20 minutes
Chill Time: 1 hour

Dijonnaise Potato Salad

**1 cup HELLMANN'S® or BEST FOODS® Real or Light
   Mayonnaise or Low Fat Mayonnaise Dressing
2 tablespoons HELLMANN'S® or BEST FOODS®
   DIJONNAISE™ Creamy Mustard
2 tablespoons chopped fresh dill *or* 1½ teaspoons dried
   dillweed
½ teaspoon salt
¼ teaspoon freshly ground pepper
1½ pounds small red potatoes, cooked and quartered
1 cup sliced radishes
½ cup chopped green onions**

1. In large bowl, combine mayonnaise, creamy mustard, dill, salt and pepper.

2. Stir in potatoes, radishes and green onions.

3. Cover; chill.   *Makes about 8 servings*

*Top to bottom: Dijonnaise Potato Salad and
Classic Potato Salad (page 102)*

Grilled Tri-Colored Pepper Salad

1 *each* large red, yellow and green bell pepper, cut into halves or quarters
⅓ cup extra-virgin olive oil
3 tablespoons balsamic vinegar
2 cloves garlic, minced
¼ teaspoon salt
¼ teaspoon black pepper
⅓ cup crumbled goat cheese (about 1½ ounces)
¼ cup thinly sliced fresh basil leaves

1. Prepare barbecue grill for direct cooking.

2. Place bell peppers, skin sides down, on grid. Grill bell peppers on covered grill, over hot coals, 10 to 12 minutes or until skin is charred. Place charred bell peppers in paper bag. Close bag; set aside to cool 10 to 15 minutes. Remove skin with paring knife; discard skin.

3. Place bell peppers in shallow glass serving dish. Combine oil, vinegar, garlic, salt and black pepper in small bowl; whisk until well combined. Pour over bell peppers. Let stand 30 minutes at room temperature. (Or, cover and refrigerate up to 24 hours. Bring bell peppers to room temperature before serving.)

4. Sprinkle bell peppers with cheese and basil just before serving.   *Makes 4 to 6 servings*

Grilled Tri-Colored Pepper Salad

Apple Cabbage Slaw

⅓ cup plain lowfat yogurt
2 tablespoons pineapple or apple juice
¼ teaspoon prepared mustard
⅛ teaspoon celery seed
3 cups shredded cabbage
2 cups diced Washington Red Delicious or Winesap apples
1 cup diagonally sliced celery
½ cup thinly sliced onion

In large bowl, whisk together yogurt, juice, mustard and celery seed. Add cabbage, apples, celery and onion. Gently toss to blend.   *Makes 4 servings*

Favorite recipe from **Washington Apple Commission**

Classic Potato Salad

1 cup HELLMANN'S® or BEST FOODS® Real or Light
   Mayonnaise or Low Fat Mayonnaise Dressing
2 tablespoons vinegar
1½ teaspoons salt
1 teaspoon sugar
¼ teaspoon freshly ground pepper
5 to 6 medium potatoes, peeled, cubed and cooked
1 cup sliced celery
½ cup chopped onion
2 hard-cooked eggs, diced

1. In large bowl, combine mayonnaise, vinegar, salt, sugar and pepper.

2. Add potatoes, celery, onion and eggs; toss to coat well.

3. Cover; chill to blend flavors.   *Makes about 8 servings*

Garden Party Pasta Salad

1 package (16 ounces) multicolor rotini
1 package (8 ounces) refrigerated tricolor tortellini
2½ cups cauliflowerets or broccoli flowerets
1 cup diced carrots
1 cup diced green bell pepper
1 cup sliced ripe olives
1 cup frozen green peas
½ cup chopped green onions
1 tablespoon dried oregano
1 tablespoon dried basil
1 jar (26 ounces) NEWMAN'S OWN® Diavolo Sauce
¾ cup NEWMAN'S OWN® Olive Oil & Vinegar Salad Dressing

Cook pastas according to package directions; drain.

Mix together pastas, cauliflower, carrots, bell pepper, olives, peas and green onions in large salad bowl.

Sprinkle oregano and basil over pasta mixture. Add Newman's Own® Diavolo Sauce and Olive Oil & Vinegar Salad Dressing; toss and refrigerate at least 3 hours.

Makes 15 to 20 side-dish servings

NOTE: May be made a day ahead.

Grilled Steak Caesar Salad

½ cup A.1.® Original or A.1.® BOLD & SPICY Steak Sauce
3 tablespoons lemon juice
1 teaspoon minced anchovy fillets
1 teaspoon minced garlic
½ cup olive oil
1 (1-pound) beef top round steak, about 1 inch thick
4 (1-inch-thick) slices French bread
4 cups torn romaine lettuce leaves
2 ounces shaved Parmesan cheese

Blend steak sauce, juice, anchovies and garlic; slowly whisk in oil until well blended. Place steak in nonmetal dish; coat with ⅓ cup steak sauce mixture. Cover; refrigerate 1 hour, turning occasionally. Reserve remaining steak sauce mixture for dressing.

Remove steak from marinade; discard marinade. Grill steak over medium-high heat 6 minutes on each side or to desired doneness. Lightly brush cut sides of bread with some reserved dressing. Grill bread 2 to 3 minutes on each side or until golden.

Heat remaining reserved dressing in small saucepan until warm. Arrange lettuce on serving platter. Thinly slice steak; arrange on lettuce. Drizzle with warm dressing; top with cheese. Serve immediately with grilled bread.   *Makes 4 servings*

Grilled Steak Caesar Salad

Roasted Pepper and Parmesan Salad with Basil Vinaigrette

1 red bell pepper
1 green bell pepper
8 small or 4 large Belgian endive
4 arugula leaves or watercress sprigs
½ cup shaved or grated Parmesan cheese
¼ cup FILIPPO BERIO® Olive Oil
2 tablespoons balsamic vinegar
1 tablespoon chopped fresh basil *or* ½ teaspoon dried basil leaves
Salt and freshly ground black pepper

Place bell peppers on baking sheet. Broil, 4 to 5 inches from heat, 5 minutes on each side or until entire surface of each bell pepper is blistered and blackened slightly. Place bell peppers in paper bag. Close bag; cool 15 to 20 minutes. Cut around cores of bell peppers; twist and remove. Cut bell peppers lengthwise in half. Peel off skins with paring knife; rinse under cold water to remove seeds. Slice bell peppers into strips. Peel leaves from endive; rinse under cold water and pat dry. Arrange endive in spoke-like fashion on 4 plates. Top with bell peppers and arugula.

Sprinkle with cheese. In small bowl, whisk together olive oil, vinegar and basil. Drizzle over endive mixture. Season to taste with salt and black pepper.   *Makes 4 servings*

Grilled Chicken Caesar Salad

1¼ cups WISH-BONE® Classic Caesar Dressing*
1 tablespoon lemon juice
1 tablespoon chopped fresh basil leaves *or* 1 teaspoon dried basil leaves
4 boneless, skinless chicken breast halves (about 1 pound)
1 large head romaine or green leaf lettuce, torn into bite-sized pieces (about 16 ounces)
2 cups croutons
Grated Parmesan cheese (optional)

Also terrific with WISH-BONE® Robusto Italian, Italian or Lite Italian Dressing.

For marinade, combine ¾ cup Classic Caesar dressing, lemon juice and basil. In large, shallow nonaluminum baking dish or plastic bag, add chicken and ⅓ cup of the marinade; turn to coat. Cover, or close bag, and marinate in refrigerator, turning occasionally, up to 3 hours. Refrigerate remaining ⅓ cup marinade.

Remove chicken, discarding marinade. Grill or broil chicken, turning once and brushing occasionally with refrigerated marinade, until chicken is done.

Meanwhile, evenly divide lettuce and croutons on 4 plates. Slice and arrange 1 chicken breast on top of each salad. Evenly drizzle with remaining ½ cup Classic Caesar Dressing. Sprinkle with cheese. *Makes 4 servings*

Gourmet Deli Potato & Pea Salad

1½ pounds new potatoes, scrubbed and quartered
1 cup water
¾ teaspoon salt, divided
½ pound sugar snap peas or snow peas, trimmed
⅓ cup reduced fat mayonnaise
⅓ cup plain nonfat yogurt
3 tablespoons FRENCH'S® Dijon Mustard
⅓ cup finely chopped red onion
2 tablespoons minced fresh dill _or_ 2 teaspoons dried dill weed
1 clove garlic, minced

Place potatoes, water and ½ teaspoon salt in 3-quart microwave-safe baking dish. Cover and microwave on HIGH (100%) 15 minutes or until potatoes are tender, stirring once. Add peas. Cover and microwave on HIGH 3 minutes or until peas are crisp-tender. Rinse with cold water and drain. Cool completely.

Combine mayonnaise, yogurt, mustard, onion, dill, garlic and remaining ¼ teaspoon salt in large bowl; mix well. Add potatoes and peas; toss to coat evenly. Cover and refrigerate 1 hour before serving. Garnish as desired.   _Makes 6 side-dish servings_

Prep Time: 15 minutes
Cook Time: 18 minutes
Chill Time: 1 hour

Gourmet Deli Potato & Pea Salad

Veggies on the Grill

Grilled Asparagus and New Potatoes

1 pound small red potatoes, scrubbed and quartered
¼ cup FRENCH'S® Classic Yellow® or Dijon Mustard
3 tablespoons minced fresh dill *or* 2 teaspoons dried dill weed
3 tablespoons olive oil
3 tablespoons lemon juice
1 tablespoon grated lemon peel
⅛ teaspoon black pepper
1 pound asparagus, washed and trimmed

1. Place potatoes and ¼ cup water in shallow microwavable dish. Cover and microwave on HIGH (100%) 8 minutes or until potatoes are crisp-tender, turning once. Drain.

2. Combine mustard, dill, oil, lemon juice, lemon peel and pepper in small bowl. Brush mixture on potatoes and asparagus. Place vegetables in grilling basket. Grill over medium-high heat 8 minutes or until potatoes and asparagus are fork-tender, turning and basting often with mustard mixture.

Makes 4 servings

Prep Time: 15 minutes
Cook Time: 16 minutes

Mesquite Summer Vegetable Medley

2 red potatoes, cut into thin wedges
2 medium carrots, diagonally sliced
3 zucchini, diagonally sliced
1 medium onion, cut into chunks
1 small head cauliflower, broken into flowerettes
½ cup LAWRY'S® Mesquite Marinade with Lime Juice
¾ teaspoon LAWRY'S® Lemon Pepper
½ teaspoon LAWRY'S® Garlic Powder with Parsley
2 bacon slices, cooked and crumbled

In large bowl, combine all ingredients except bacon; mix well. Place vegetable mixture evenly on 4 (20×12-inch) pieces heavy-duty aluminum foil. Fold foil to enclose; seal tightly. Grill packets seam side up 20 to 30 minutes or until vegetables are tender. To serve, carefully remove vegetables—they will be very hot. Sprinkle with bacon. *Makes 4 servings*

SERVING SUGGESTION: Serve with grilled meat, chicken or fish.

Grilled Vegetables al Fresco

2 large red bell peppers
2 medium zucchini
1 large eggplant

Spicy Marinade
⅔ cup white wine vinegar
½ cup soy sauce
2 tablespoons minced ginger
2 tablespoons olive oil
2 tablespoons sesame oil
2 large cloves garlic, minced
2 teaspoons TABASCO® brand Pepper Sauce

Seed red peppers; cut each pepper into quarters. Cut each zucchini lengthwise into ¼-inch-thick strips. Slice eggplant into ¼-inch-thick rounds.

In 13×9-inch baking dish, combine Spicy Marinade ingredients. Place vegetable pieces in mixture; toss to mix well. Cover and refrigerate vegetables at least 2 hours and up to 24 hours, turning occasionally.

About 30 minutes before serving, preheat grill to medium heat, placing rack 5 to 6 inches above coals. Place red peppers, zucchini and eggplant slices on grill rack. Grill vegetables 4 minutes, turning once and brushing with marinade occasionally.

Makes 4 servings

Grilled Cajun Potato Wedges

3 large russet potatoes, washed and scrubbed (do not peel)
  (about 2¼ pounds)
¼ cup olive oil
2 cloves garlic, minced
1 teaspoon salt
1 teaspoon paprika
½ teaspoon dried thyme leaves
½ teaspoon dried oregano leaves
¼ teaspoon black pepper
⅛ to ¼ teaspoon ground red pepper
2 cups mesquite chips

1. Prepare barbecue grill for direct cooking. Preheat oven to 425°F. Cut potatoes in half lengthwise; then cut each half lengthwise into 4 wedges. Place potatoes in large bowl. Add oil and garlic; toss to coat well.

2. Combine salt, paprika, thyme, oregano, black pepper and ground red pepper in small bowl. Sprinkle over potatoes; toss to coat well. Place potato wedges in single layer in shallow roasting pan. (Reserve remaining oil mixture left in large bowl.) Bake 20 minutes. Remove potato wedges from oven; cover to keep warm.

3. Meanwhile, cover mesquite chips with cold water; soak 20 minutes. Drain mesquite chips; sprinkle over coals. Place potato wedges on their sides on grid. Grill covered, over medium coals, 15 to 20 minutes or until potatoes are browned and fork-tender, brushing with reserved oil mixture halfway through grilling time and turning once with tongs.

Makes 4 to 6 servings

Grilled Cajun Potato Wedges

Honey-Grilled Vegetables

12 small red potatoes, halved
¼ cup honey
3 tablespoons dry white wine
1 clove garlic, minced
1 teaspoon dried thyme leaves
½ teaspoon salt
½ teaspoon black pepper
2 zucchini, halved lengthwise and cut crosswise into halves
1 medium eggplant, sliced ½ inch thick
1 green bell pepper, cut vertically in eighths
1 red bell pepper, cut vertically in eighths
1 large onion, sliced ½ inch thick

Cover potatoes with water. Bring to a boil and simmer 5 minutes; drain. Combine honey, wine, garlic, thyme, salt and black pepper; mix well. Place vegetables on oiled barbecue grill over hot coals. Grill 20 to 25 minutes, turning and brushing with honey mixture every 7 or 8 minutes.   *Makes 4 to 6 servings*

OVEN METHOD: Toss vegetables with honey mixture. Bake, uncovered, at 400°F 25 minutes or until tender; mix every 8 to 10 minutes to prevent burning.

Favorite recipe from **National Honey Board**

Honey-Grilled Vegetables

Grilled Stuffed Eggplant

4 baby eggplant (1½ pounds)*
2 tablespoons olive oil
**4 ounces small mushrooms, wiped clean and quartered
    (about 1 cup)**
½ cup finely chopped green and/or red bell pepper
2 cloves garlic, minced
1 cup chunky-style salsa
**1⅓ cups *FRENCH'S*® *Taste Toppers*™ *French Fried Onions*,
    divided**
2 tablespoons crumbled goat cheese
1 tablespoon grated Parmesan cheese

**You may substitute 2 medium eggplant (1½ pounds) for the baby eggplant.
Cut eggplant in half lengthwise; proceed as directed.*

Cut lengthwise slice ½ inch from top of each eggplant; discard.
Using a spoon or melon baller, scoop out pulp, leaving ¼-inch
shell. Set aside eggplant shells. Finely chop pulp.

Heat oil in large skillet over high heat. Add eggplant pulp and
mushrooms; cook about 5 minutes or until liquid is evaporated,
stirring often. Add pepper and garlic; cook and stir until pepper
is tender. Stir in salsa. Bring to a boil. Reduce heat to medium.
Cook and stir 2 minutes. Stir in ⅔ cup **Taste Toppers**. Spoon
filling into shells, mounding slightly. Sprinkle remaining ⅔ *cup*
onions and cheeses on top.

Place eggplant on oiled grid. Grill over medium coals 15 minutes
or until eggplant shells are tender. Serve warm.

Makes 4 side-dish servings

Jamaican Grilled Sweet Potatoes

2 large (about 1½ pounds) sweet potatoes or yams
3 tablespoons packed brown sugar
2 tablespoons softened margarine, divided
1 teaspoon ground ginger
1 tablespoon chopped fresh cilantro
2 teaspoons dark rum

1. Pierce potatoes in several places with fork. Place on paper towel in microwave. Microwave at HIGH 5 to 6 minutes or until crisp-tender, rotating ¼ turn halfway through cooking. Let stand 10 minutes. Diagonally slice about ½ inch off ends of potatoes. Continue cutting potatoes diagonally into ¾-inch-thick slices.

2. Combine brown sugar, 1 tablespoon margarine and ginger in small bowl; mix well. Stir in cilantro and rum; set aside.

3. Melt remaining 1 tablespoon margarine. With half of melted margarine, lightly brush one side of each potato slice. Grill slices, margarine sides down, on covered grill, over medium coals, 4 to 6 minutes or until grillmarked. Brush tops with remaining melted margarine; turn over and grill 3 to 5 minutes or until grillmarked. Spoon rum mixture equally over potato slices before serving. *Makes 6 servings*

Prep and Cook Time: 30 minutes

Grilled Coriander Corn

4 ears fresh corn
3 tablespoons butter or margarine, softened
1 teaspoon ground coriander
¼ teaspoon salt
⅛ teaspoon ground red pepper

1. Pull outer husks from top to base of each corn; leave husks attached to ear. Strip away silk from corn.

2. Place corn in large bowl. Cover with cold water; soak 20 to 30 minutes.

3. Meanwhile, prepare grill for direct cooking.

4. Remove corn from water; pat kernels dry with paper towels. Combine butter, coriander, salt and ground red pepper in small bowl. Brush butter mixture over kernels.

5. Bring husks back up each ear of corn; secure at top with wet string.

6. Place corn on grid. Grill corn on covered grill, over medium-hot coals, 20 to 25 minutes or until corn is hot and tender, turning with tongs halfway through grilling time.

Makes 4 servings

Grilled Coriander Corn

Portobello Mushrooms Sesame

4 large portobello mushrooms
2 tablespoons sweet rice wine
2 tablespoons reduced-sodium soy sauce
2 cloves garlic, minced
1 teaspoon dark sesame oil

1. Remove and discard stems from mushrooms; set caps aside. Combine remaining ingredients in small bowl.

2. Brush both sides of mushrooms with soy sauce mixture. Grill mushrooms, top sides up, on covered grill, over medium coals, 3 to 4 minutes. Brush tops with soy sauce mixture and turn over; grill 2 minutes more or until mushrooms are lightly browned. Turn again and grill, basting frequently, 4 to 5 minutes or until tender when pressed with back of spatula. Remove mushrooms and cut diagonally into ½-inch-thick slices.

Makes 4 servings

Portobello Mushrooms Sesame

Savory Herb-Stuffed Onions

1 zucchini, cut lengthwise into ¼-inch-thick slices
  Nonstick cooking spray
3 shiitake mushrooms
4 large sweet onions
1 plum tomato, seeded and chopped
2 tablespoons fresh bread crumbs
1 tablespoon fresh basil *or* 1 teaspoon dried basil leaves
1 teaspoon olive oil
¼ teaspoon salt
⅛ teaspoon black pepper
4 teaspoons balsamic vinegar

1. Spray both sides of zucchini with cooking spray. Grill on uncovered grill over medium coals 4 minutes or until tender, turning once. Cool; cut into bite-size pieces.

2. Thread mushrooms onto metal skewers. Grill on covered grill, over medium coals, 20 to 30 minutes or until tender. Remove mushrooms from skewers and coarsely chop; set aside.

3. Remove stem and root ends of onions, leaving peels intact. Spray onions with cooking spray; grill, root ends up, on covered grill over medium coals 5 minutes or until lightly charred. Remove; cool slightly. Peel and scoop about 1 inch of pulp from stem ends; chop pulp for filling.

4. Combine chopped onion, mushrooms, zucchini, tomato, bread crumbs, basil, oil, salt and pepper; mix until well blended. Spoon equal amounts of stuffing mixture into centers of onions. *Makes 4 appetizer servings*

Zesty Corn-on-the-Cob

6 ears fresh corn
¼ cup butter or margarine, melted
1 tablespoon chopped fresh parsley
2 teaspoons prepared horseradish
¼ teaspoon paprika
¼ teaspoon black pepper
⅛ teaspoon salt

1. Pull outer husks from top to base of each corn ear; leave husks attached to ear. Strip away silk. Trim any blemishes from corn. Place corn in large bowl. Cover with cold water; soak 20 to 30 minutes.

2. Prepare grill for direct cooking.

3. Remove corn from water; pat kernels dry with paper towels. Combine butter, parsley, horseradish, paprika, pepper and salt in small bowl. Spread about half of margarine mixture evenly over kernels.

4. Bring husks back up each ear of corn; secure at top with wet string. Place corn on grid. Grill, covered, over medium-high heat 15 to 20 minutes or until corn is hot and tender, turning every 5 minutes.

5. Transfer corn to serving plate. Remove front half of husks on each piece of corn; brush with remaining butter mixture.

Makes 6 servings

Grilled Sweet Potatoes

4 medium-sized sweet potatoes (2 pounds), peeled
⅓ cup FRENCH'S® Dijon Mustard
2 tablespoons olive oil
1 tablespoon minced fresh rosemary *or* 1 teaspoon dried
    rosemary
½ teaspoon salt
¼ teaspoon black pepper

1. Cut potatoes diagonally into ½-inch-thick slices. Place potatoes and 1 cup water in shallow microwavable dish. Cover with vented plastic wrap and microwave on HIGH (100%) 6 minutes or until potatoes are crisp-tender, turning once. (Cook potatoes in two batches, if necessary.) Drain well.

2. Combine mustard, oil, rosemary, salt and pepper in small bowl; brush on potato slices. Place potatoes on oiled grid. Grill over medium-high heat 5 to 8 minutes or until potatoes are fork-tender, turning and basting often with mustard mixture.

Makes 4 servings

TIP: The task of selecting sweet potatoes is an easy one. Just look for medium-sized potatoes with thick, dark-orange skins that are free from bruises. Sweet potatoes keep best in a dry, dark area at about 55°F. Under these conditions they should last about 3 to 4 weeks.

Prep Time: 15 minutes
Cook Time: 18 minutes

Grilled Sweet Potatoes

BASTE IT!

Oriental Steak Marinade

1 cup A.1.® THICK & HEARTY Steak Sauce
¼ cup sherry cooking wine
¼ cup finely chopped red bell pepper
3 tablespoons firmly packed light brown sugar
3 tablespoons soy sauce
1 tablespoon Oriental sesame oil
2 cloves garlic, minced

In small nonmetal bowl, combine steak sauce, sherry, pepper, sugar, soy sauce, oil and garlic. Use to marinate any steak about 1 hour in refrigerator.

Remove steak from marinade; reserve marinade. Grill or broil steak to desired doneness. Meanwhile, in small saucepan, over high heat, bring reserved marinade to a boil; simmer 5 minutes or until thickened. Serve steak with warm sauce.

Makes 1⅔ cups

Baste It!

Firehouse Marinated Steak

¼ cup **WESSON® Best Blend or Vegetable Oil**
6 **dried pasilla or ancho chilies, seeded and cut into strips**
1 **cup coarsely chopped onion**
1½ **teaspoons chopped fresh garlic**
½ **cup beef broth**
2 **tablespoons fresh lime juice**
2 **teaspoons cumin seed**
1½ **teaspoons salt**
1 **teaspoon brown sugar**
4 **New York steaks** *or* 1 **(2-pound) flank steak, tenderized lightly with meat mallet**
2 **limes**

In a medium skillet, heat Wesson® Oil over medium-low heat. Add chilies, onion and garlic; sauté until onion is tender. *Do not drain.* Pour onion mixture into blender. Add *remaining* ingredients *except* steaks and limes; blend until smooth. If marinade is too thick, add additional beef broth. Place steaks in large resealable plastic food storage bag. Pour half the marinade over steaks; set aside *remaining* marinade. Seal bag and turn to coat. Marinate in refrigerator for 30 minutes. Bring steaks to room temperature. Over hot coals, grill steaks while basting with ¾ of reserved marinade. Grill to desired doneness. Before serving, brush beef with *remaining* ¼ marinade and generously squeeze fresh lime juice over steaks. *Makes 4 servings*

TIP: This spicy marinade can be made up to 3 days ahead of time; the flavors improve with age.

Firehouse Marinated Steak

Curried Barbecue Sauce

¼ **cup chopped green onions**
1 **clove garlic, minced**
1 **tablespoon vegetable oil**
1 **teaspoon curry powder**
⅓ **cup A.1.® Original or A.1.® BOLD & SPICY Steak Sauce**
⅓ **cup GREY POUPON® Dijon Mustard**
½ **cup plain low fat yogurt**

Sauté green onions and garlic in oil in small saucepan over low heat until tender. Stir in curry; cook 1 minute. Stir in steak sauce and mustard. Remove saucepan from heat; cool slightly. Stir in yogurt. Use as a basting sauce while grilling or broiling steak. *Makes about 1⅓ cups*

Moroccan Charmoula Marinade

½ cup fresh cilantro
½ to 1 jalapeño pepper,* stemmed and seeded, *or* ⅛ to
   ¼ teaspoon ground red pepper
 2 tablespoons white wine vinegar or rice vinegar
 1 tablespoon minced fresh ginger
 3 cloves garlic, minced
 2 teaspoons grated fresh lemon peel
 1 teaspoon cumin seeds
 1 teaspoon paprika
 ¼ cup fresh lemon juice

Jalapeño peppers can sting and irritate the skin; wear rubber gloves when handling peppers and do not touch eyes. Wash hands after handling peppers.

Place cilantro, jalapeño, vinegar, ginger, garlic, lemon peel, cumin and paprika in food processor or blender and process until finely chopped. Add lemon juice* and process until blended.   *Makes 8 servings*

If using a blender, add only as much lemon juice to mixture as needed to finely chop ingredients, then add remaining juice. Alternatively, mince fresh ingredients by hand, then stir in vinegar and lemon juice; use ground cumin in place of cumin seeds.

Citrus Grove Marinated Salmon

4 salmon fillets or steaks
⅓ cup lemonade concentrate, thawed
¼ cup WESSON® Vegetable Oil
¼ cup orange juice concentrate, thawed
½ tablespoon fresh dill weed *or* ½ teaspoon dried dill weed
WESSON® No-Stick Cooking Spray

1. Rinse salmon and pat dry; set aside.

2. In a small bowl, combine *remaining* ingredients *except* Wesson Cooking Spray.

3. Place salmon in a large resealable plastic food storage bag; pour ¾ marinade over fish; set *remaining* marinade aside. Seal bag and gently turn to coat; refrigerate 2 hours, turning fish several times during marinating.

4. Preheat broiler. Foil-line jelly roll pan; spray with Wesson Cooking Spray.

5. Place fish on pan; discard used marinade. Broil fish until it flakes easily with a fork, basting frequently with *remaining* marinade and once before serving.

Makes 4 (6-ounce) servings

Citrus Grove Marinated Salmon

Marinated Italian Sausage and Peppers

½ **cup olive oil**
¼ **cup red wine vinegar**
 2 **tablespoons chopped fresh parsley**
 1 **tablespoon dried oregano leaves**
 2 **cloves garlic, crushed**
 1 **teaspoon salt**
 1 **teaspoon black pepper**
 4 **hot or sweet Italian sausage links**
 1 **large onion, sliced into rings**
 1 **large bell pepper, sliced into quarters**
   Horseradish-Mustard Spread (page 138)

Combine oil, vinegar, parsley, oregano, garlic, salt and black pepper in small bowl. Place sausages, onion and bell pepper in large resealable plastic food storage bag; pour oil mixture into bag. Close bag securely, turning to coat. Marinate in refrigerator 1 to 2 hours.

Prepare Horseradish-Mustard Spread; set aside. Prepare grill for direct cooking. Drain sausages, onion and bell pepper; reserve marinade.

Grill sausages, covered, 4 to 5 minutes. Turn sausages and place onion and bell pepper on grid. Brush sausages and vegetables with reserved marinade. Grill, covered, 5 minutes or until vegetables are crisp-tender, turning vegetables halfway through grilling time. Serve sausages, onions and bell peppers with Horseradish-Mustard Spread. *Makes 4 servings*

continued on page 138

Marinated Italian Sausage and Peppers

Baste It!

Marinated Italian Sausage and Peppers, continued

Horseradish-Mustard Spread

3 tablespoons mayonnaise
1 tablespoon Dijon mustard
1 tablespoon prepared horseradish
1 tablespoon chopped fresh parsley
2 teaspoons garlic powder
1 teaspoon black pepper

Combine all ingredients in small bowl; mix well.

Makes about ½ cup

Mexicana Marinade Paste

1 package (1.0 ounce) LAWRY'S® Taco Spices & Seasonings
1 tablespoon lime juice
1 tablespoon vegetable oil
4 boneless, skinless chicken breast halves (about 1 pound)

In small bowl, combine Taco Spices & Seasonings, lime juice and oil; mix well. Brush mixture on both sides of chicken. Grill or broil chicken 10 to 15 minutes or until no longer pink in center and juices run clear when cut, turning halfway through grilling time.

Makes 4 servings

SERVING SUGGESTION: Serve with Mexican rice and black beans. Guacamole and chips would complement the meal as well.

HINT: This paste can also be used on beef or pork.

Balsamic Marinade

2 pounds beef, pork, lamb or veal
½ cup FILIPPO BERIO® Olive Oil
½ cup balsamic vinegar
2 cloves garlic, slivered
1 teaspoon dried oregano leaves
½ teaspoon salt
½ teaspoon dried marjoram leaves
¼ teaspoon freshly ground pepper

Place meat in shallow glass dish. In small bowl, whisk together olive oil, vinegar, garlic, oregano, salt, marjoram and pepper. Pour marinade over meat, using about ½ cup for each pound of meat. Turn to coat both sides. Cover; marinate several hours or overnight, turning meat occasionally. Remove meat; boil marinade 1 minute. Grill meat, brushing frequently with marinade. *Makes 1 cup marinade*

Rib Ticklin' Barbecue Sauce

½ cup KARO® Light or Dark Corn Syrup
½ cup ketchup
½ cup finely chopped onion
¼ cup cider vinegar
¼ cup prepared mustard
¼ cup Worcestershire sauce

1. In 1½-quart saucepan combine corn syrup, ketchup, onion, vinegar, mustard and Worcestershire sauce. Stirring frequently, bring to boil over medium-high heat. Reduce heat; boil gently 15 minutes or until thickened.

2. Brush on chicken, ribs or beef during last 15 to 20 minutes of grilling, turning frequently. Heat remaining sauce to serve with meat.   *Makes about 2 cups*

Prep Time: 25 minutes

Rib Ticklin' Barbecue Sauce

Leg of Lamb with Wine Marinade

1½ cups red wine
1 onion, chopped
1 carrot, chopped
1 rib celery, chopped
2 tablespoons chopped fresh parsley
2 tablespoons olive oil
3 cloves garlic, minced
1 tablespoon dried thyme leaves
1 teaspoon salt
1 teaspoon black pepper
1½ pounds boneless leg of lamb, trimmed

Combine all ingredients, except lamb, in medium bowl. Place lamb in large resealable plastic food storage bag. Add wine mixture to bag. Close bag securely, turning to coat. Marinate in refrigerator 2 hours or overnight.

Prepare grill for indirect cooking. Drain lamb; reserve marinade.

Place lamb on grid directly over drip pan. Grill covered, over medium heat, about 45 minutes for medium or until internal temperature reaches 145°F when tested with meat thermometer inserted into thickest part of roast, not touching bone. Brush occasionally with reserved marinade. (Do not brush with marinade during last 5 minutes of grilling.)

Transfer roast to cutting board; let stand 10 to 15 minutes before carving. Internal temperature will continue to rise 5°F to 10°F during stand time.   *Makes 4 servings*

Leg of Lamb with Wine Marinade

Lime-Mustard Marinated Chicken

2 boneless skinless chicken breast halves (about 3 ounces each)
¼ cup fresh lime juice
3 tablespoons honey mustard, divided
2 teaspoons olive oil
¼ teaspoon ground cumin
⅛ teaspoon garlic powder
⅛ teaspoon ground red pepper
¾ cup plus 2 tablespoons fat-free reduced-sodium chicken broth, divided
¼ cup uncooked rice
1 cup broccoli florets
⅓ cup matchstick carrots

1. Rinse chicken. Pat dry with paper towels. Place in resealable plastic food storage bag. Whisk together lime juice, 2 tablespoons mustard, olive oil, cumin, garlic powder and red pepper. Pour over chicken. Seal bag. Marinate in refrigerator 2 hours.

2. Combine ¾ cup chicken broth, rice and remaining 1 tablespoon mustard in small saucepan. Bring to a boil. Reduce heat and simmer, covered, 12 minutes or until rice is almost tender. Stir in broccoli, carrots, and remaining 2 tablespoons chicken broth. Cook, covered, 2 to 3 minutes more or until vegetables are crisp-tender and rice is tender.

3. Meanwhile, drain chicken; discard marinade. Prepare grill for direct grilling. Grill chicken over medium coals 10 to 13 minutes or until no longer pink in center. Serve chicken with rice mixture. *Makes 2 servings*

Lime-Mustard Marinated Chicken

HAPPY ENDINGS

Strawberry Yogurt Tarts

1 (8-ounce) carton strawberry yogurt
2 cups COOL WHIP® Whipped Topping, thawed, divided
1 (4-ounce) package KEEBLER® Ready Crust® Single Serve
   Graham Crusts
1 pint fresh strawberries, cut into halves

1. In small bowl, blend yogurt and 1 cup whipped topping.

2. Spoon yogurt mixture evenly into crusts. Arrange
2 strawberry halves around yogurt on each tart.

3. Garnish with remaining 1 cup whipped topping. Chill 1 hour
or until firm.   *Makes 6 tarts*

Preparation Time: 15 minutes
Chilling Time: 1 hour

Almond-Pumpkin Chiffon Pudding

1 envelope unflavored gelatin
1 cup 2% low-fat milk
1 cup solid pack pumpkin
½ teaspoon pumpkin pie spice
1 container (8 ounces) plain low fat yogurt
3 egg whites
Dash salt
⅔ cup packed brown sugar
½ cup chopped toasted California Almonds, divided

Sprinkle gelatin over milk in small saucepan; let stand 5 minutes to soften. Cook and stir constantly over low heat until gelatin dissolves; remove from heat. Stir in pumpkin and pumpkin pie spice. Cool to room temperature; stir in yogurt. Refrigerate until mixture begins to thicken and gel. Beat egg whites with salt to form soft peaks. Gradually beat in brown sugar, beating to form stiff peaks; fold into pumpkin mixture. Sprinkle 1 tablespoon almonds over bottom of greased 6-cup mold. Fold remaining almonds into pumpkin mixture; spoon into mold. Refrigerate until firm. Unmold to serve.   *Makes 8 servings*

Favorite recipe from **Almond Board of California**

Fudgy Milk Chocolate Fondue

1 (16-ounce) can chocolate-flavored syrup
1 (14-ounce) can EAGLE® BRAND Sweetened Condensed
    Milk (NOT evaporated milk)
    Dash salt
1½ teaspoons vanilla extract
    Dippers: fresh fruit, cookies, pound cake cubes, angel
    food cake cubes

1. In heavy saucepan over medium heat, combine syrup, **Eagle Brand** and salt. Cook and stir 12 to 15 minutes or until slightly thickened.

2. Remove from heat; stir in vanilla. Serve warm with Dippers. Store covered in refrigerator.   *Makes about 3 cups*

MICROWAVE DIRECTIONS: In 1-quart glass measure, combine syrup, **Eagle Brand** and salt. Microwave at HIGH 3½ to 4 minutes, stirring after 2 minutes. Stir in vanilla.

TIP: Can be served warm or cold over ice cream. Can be made several weeks ahead. Store tightly covered in refrigerator.

Prep Time: 12 to 15 minutes

Sunny Peach Trifle

   2 cups cold milk
  ¾ cup sugar
   2 tablespoons cornstarch
   4 egg yolks, beaten
 1½ teaspoons vanilla
2½ cups whipped topping, divided
   4 medium peaches, peeled and sliced
   2 packages (3 ounces each) ladyfingers
  ¼ cup rum
   2 cups raspberries

Combine milk, sugar and cornstarch in top of double boiler. Stir until combined; cover. Cook over boiling water 7 minutes; do not stir. Uncover; cook and stir 10 minutes. Add ⅓ milk mixture to egg yolks; blend well. Add egg mixture to remaining milk mixture; blend well. Cook 2 minutes, stirring constantly. Remove from heat; stir in vanilla. Cool completely. Fold 1½ cups whipped topping into custard; cover and chill.

Reserve several peach slices for garnish. Layer ⅓ of ladyfingers in deep dish. Sprinkle with ⅓ of rum. Top with ⅓ of custard, peaches and berries. Repeat layers, ending with custard. Refrigerate until ready to serve. Top with reserved peach slices and remaining whipped topping.   *Makes 8 to 10 servings*

Sunny Peach Trifle

Watermelon Ice

4 cups seeded 1-inch watermelon chunks
¼ cup thawed frozen unsweetened pineapple juice
concentrate
2 tablespoons fresh lime juice
Fresh melon balls (optional)
Fresh mint leaves (optional)

Place melon chunks in single layer in plastic freezer bag; freeze until firm, about 8 hours. Place frozen melon in food processor container fitted with steel blade. Let stand 15 minutes to soften slightly. Add pineapple juice and lime juice. Remove plunger from top of food processor to allow air to be incorporated. Process until smooth, scraping down sides of container frequently. Spoon into individual dessert dishes. Garnish with melon balls and mint leaves, if desired. Freeze leftovers.

Makes 6 servings

HONEYDEW ICE: Substitute honeydew for watermelon and unsweetened pineapple-guava-orange juice concentrate for pineapple juice concentrate.

CANTALOUPE ICE: Substitute cantaloupe for watermelon and unsweetened pineapple-guava-orange juice concentrate for pineapple juice concentrate.

NOTE: Ices may be transferred to airtight container and frozen up to 1 month. Let stand at room temperature 10 minutes to soften slightly before serving.

Watemelon Ice, Honeydew Ice and Cantaloupe Ice

Cappuccino Bars

15 whole chocolate graham crackers, divided
2 packages (8 ounces each) PHILADELPHIA® Cream
    Cheese, softened
3½ cups cold milk
3 packages (4-serving size each) JELL-O® Chocolate Flavor
    Instant Pudding & Pie Filling
1 tablespoon MAXWELL HOUSE® Instant Coffee
¼ teaspoon ground cinnamon
1 tub (8 ounces) COOL WHIP® Whipped Topping, thawed
1 square BAKER'S® Semi-Sweet Baking Chocolate, grated *or*
    3 tablespoons chocolate sprinkles

ARRANGE half of the crackers in bottom of 13×9-inch pan,
cutting crackers to fit, if necessary.

BEAT cream cheese in large bowl with electric mixer on low
speed until smooth. Gradually beat in 1 cup milk. Add
remaining milk, pudding mixes, instant coffee and cinnamon.
Beat 1 to 2 minutes. (Mixture will be thick.) Gently stir in 2 cups
whipped topping.

SPREAD half of the pudding mixture over crackers in pan.
Arrange remaining crackers over pudding in pan. Top with
remaining pudding mixture. Cover with remaining whipped
topping. Sprinkle with grated chocolate.

FREEZE 3 hours or overnight. Cut into bars. Garnish as desired.

Makes 18 servings

Prep Time: 10 minutes

Mango Vanilla Parfait

½ **(4-serving-size) package vanilla sugar-free instant pudding mix**
1¼ **cups fat-free (skim) milk**
½ **cup mango cubes**
2 **large strawberries, sliced**
3 **sugar-free shortbread cookies, crumbled,** *or* 2 **tablespoons reduced-fat granola**
Strawberry slices for garnish

1. Prepare pudding according to package directions using 1¼ cups milk.

2. In parfait glass or small glass bowl, layer quarter of pudding, half of mango, half of strawberries and quarter of pudding. Repeat layers in second parfait glass. Refrigerate 30 minutes.

3. Just before serving, top with cookie crumbs and garnish with strawberries. *Makes 2 servings*

Raspberry Almond Trifles

2 cups whipping cream
¼ cup plus 1 tablespoon raspberry liqueur or orange juice, divided
1 (14-ounce) can EAGLE® BRAND Sweetened Condensed Milk (NOT evaporated milk)
2 (3-ounce) packages ladyfingers, separated
1 cup seedless raspberry jam
½ cup sliced almonds, toasted

1. In large bowl, beat whipping cream and 1 tablespoon liqueur until stiff peaks form. Fold in **Eagle Brand;** set aside.

2. Layer bottom of 12 (4-ounce) custard cups or ramekins with ladyfingers. Brush with some remaining liqueur. Spread half of jam over ladyfingers. Spread evenly with half of cream mixture; sprinkle with half of almonds. Repeat layers with remaining ladyfingers, liqueur, jam, cream mixture and almonds. Cover and chill 2 hours. Store covered in refrigerator.

Makes 12 servings

Prep Time: 20 minutes
Chill Time: 2 hours

Raspberry Almond Trifles

Three-Melon Soup

3 cups cubed seeded watermelon
3 tablespoons unsweetened pineapple juice
2 tablespoons lemon juice
¼ cantaloupe melon
⅛ honeydew melon

1. Combine watermelon, pineapple juice and lemon juice in blender; process until smooth. Chill at least 2 hours or overnight.

2. Scoop out balls of cantaloupe and honeydew.

3. To serve, pour watermelon mixture into shallow bowls; garnish with cantaloupe and honeydew.   *Makes 4 servings*

Ginger Snap Sandwiches

¼ cup 1% low fat cottage cheese
¼ cup vanilla nonfat yogurt
1 McIntosh apple, peeled, cored and grated
2 tablespoons sugar
30 ginger snaps

Add cottage cheese and yogurt to food processor or blender; process until smooth. Blend in apple and sugar. Using rubber spatula, spread apple filling onto flat side of ginger snap; top with another ginger snap to make sandwich. Repeat with remaining ingredients.   *Makes 15 servings*

Favorite recipe from **The Sugar Association, Inc.**

Three-Melon Soup

Strawberry Daiquiri Dessert

**1 package (3 ounces) ladyfingers, thawed if frozen, split in
half horizontally**
2 tablespoons light rum or apricot nectar
**1 container (8 ounces) thawed nondairy whipped topping,
divided**
1 package (8 ounces) cream cheese, softened
1 package (16 ounces) frozen strawberries, thawed
**1 can (10 ounces) frozen strawberry daiquiri mix, thawed
Fresh strawberries (optional)**

Place ladyfinger halves, cut side up, in bottom of 11×7-inch
dish. Brush with rum.

Reserve 1 cup whipped topping in small bowl; refrigerate,
covered.

Place cream cheese in food processor; process until fluffy. Add
remaining whipped topping, thawed frozen strawberries and
daiquiri mix; process with on/off pulses until blended. Pour over
ladyfingers.

Freeze 6 hours or overnight. Remove from freezer. Allow dish
to stand at room temperature 20 to 30 minutes before serving.
Garnish with remaining whipped topping and fresh strawberries,
if desired. Store any leftover dessert in freezer.

Makes 10 servings

Easy Grilling

Contents

Burgers, Burgers, Burgers

America's Favorite Cheddar Beef Burgers

1 pound ground beef
⅓ cup A.1.® Steak Sauce, divided
1 medium onion, cut into strips
1 medium green or red bell pepper, cut into strips
1 tablespoon margarine or butter
4 ounces Cheddar cheese, sliced
4 hamburger rolls
4 tomato slices

Mix ground beef and 3 tablespoons steak sauce; shape mixture into 4 burgers. Set aside.

Cook and stir onion and pepper in margarine or butter in medium skillet until tender. Stir in remaining steak sauce; keep warm.

Grill burgers over medium heat for 4 minutes on each side or until done. When almost done, top with cheese; grill until cheese melts. Spoon 2 tablespoons onion mixture onto each roll bottom; top each with burger, tomato slice, some of remaining onion mixture and roll top. Serve immediately.

Makes 4 servings

Grilled Jalapeño Turkey Burgers

1 package (1¼ pounds) BUTTERBALL® Lean Fresh Ground Turkey
¼ cup chopped green onions
2 tablespoons chopped pickled jalapeño peppers or mild green chilies
1 clove garlic, minced
1 teaspoon Worcestershire sauce
½ teaspoon salt
⅛ teaspoon black pepper

Prepare grill for medium-direct-heat cooking. Lightly spray unheated grill rack with nonstick cooking spray. Combine all ingredients in large bowl; mix well. Form into six large patties. Grill 6 minutes on each side or until meat is no longer pink in center. Serve with your favorite condiments. *Makes 6 burgers*

Preparation Time: 15 minutes

BBQ Cheeseburgers

1 pound lean ground beef
¼ cup finely chopped onion
Prepared barbecue sauce
4 slices (1 ounce each) Cheddar or mozzarella cheese
4 crusty rolls, split
Romaine lettuce
Sliced tomato

1. In medium bowl, combine ground beef and onion, mixing lightly but thoroughly. Shape into four ½-inch-thick patties.

2. Place patties on grid over medium ash-covered coals. Grill uncovered 11 to 13 minutes or until centers are no longer pink, turning once. Approximately 1 minute before burgers are done, brush with barbecue sauce; top with cheese.

3. Line bottom half of each roll with lettuce and tomato; top with burger. Close sandwiches. *Makes 4 servings*

Prep & Cook Time: 30 minutes

Favorite recipe from **National Cattlemen's Beef Association**

Grilled Jalapeño Turkey Burger

Big D Ranch Burgers

 1 cup sliced onions
 ⅓ cup sliced green bell pepper strips
 ⅓ cup sliced red bell pepper strips
 1 tablespoon margarine or butter
 3 tablespoons A.1.® Steak Sauce
 2 teaspoons prepared horseradish
 1 pound ground beef
 4 onion rolls, split

Cook onions, green pepper and red pepper in margarine or butter in skillet over medium heat until tender-crisp. Stir in steak sauce and horseradish; keep warm.

Shape ground beef into 4 burgers. Grill burgers over medium heat for 5 minutes on each side or until desired doneness. Place burgers on roll bottoms; top each with ¼ cup pepper mixture and roll top. Serve immediately. *Makes 4 servings*

Tasty Taco Burgers

 1 pound ground beef
 1 package (1¼ ounces) taco seasoning mix
 8 KRAFT® American Singles Pasteurized Process Cheese Food
 4 Kaiser rolls, split
 Lettuce leaves
 Salsa
 BREAKSTONE'S® or KNUDSEN® Sour Cream (optional)

MIX 1 pound ground beef and taco seasoning mix. Shape into 4 patties.

GRILL patties over hot coals 6 to 8 minutes on each side or to desired doneness. Top each patty with 2 process cheese food slices. Continue grilling until process cheese food is melted.

FILL rolls with lettuce and cheeseburgers. Top with salsa and sour cream, if desired. *Makes 4 servings*

Hawaiian-Style Burgers

1½ pounds ground beef
⅓ cup sliced green onions
2 tablespoons Worcestershire sauce
⅛ teaspoon black pepper
⅓ cup pineapple preserves
⅓ cup barbecue sauce
6 pineapple slices
6 hamburger buns, split and toasted

1. Combine beef, onions, Worcestershire and pepper in large bowl. Shape into six 1-inch-thick patties.

2. Combine preserves and barbecue sauce in small saucepan. Bring to a boil over medium heat, stirring often.

3. Place patties on grill rack directly above medium coals. Grill, uncovered, until desired doneness, turning and brushing often with sauce mixture. Place pineapple on grill; grill 1 minute or until browned, turning once.

4. To serve, place patties on buns with pineapple.   *Makes 6 servings*

The All-American Burger

Burger Spread (recipe follows)
1½ pounds ground beef
2 tablespoons chopped fresh parsley
2 teaspoons onion powder
2 teaspoons Worcestershire sauce
1 teaspoon garlic powder
1 teaspoon salt
1 teaspoon black pepper
4 hamburger buns, split

Prepare Burger Spread; set aside.

Prepare grill for direct cooking.

Combine beef with parsley, onion powder, Worcestershire, garlic powder, salt and pepper in medium bowl; mix lightly, but thoroughly. Shape mixture into four ½-inch-thick burgers.

Place burgers on grid. Grill, covered, over medium heat 8 to 10 minutes for medium or until desired doneness is reached, turning halfway through grilling time.

Remove burgers from grill. Place burgers on buns; top each burger with Burger Spread. *Makes 4 servings*

Burger Spread

½ cup ketchup
¼ cup prepared mustard
2 tablespoons chopped onion
1 tablespoon relish or chopped pickles
1 tablespoon chopped fresh parsley

Combine all ingredients in small bowl; mix well. *Makes 1 cup*

The All-American Burger

Inside-Out Brie Burgers

1 pound ground beef
5 tablespoons A.1.® Original or A.1.® BOLD & SPICY Steak Sauce,
    divided
3 ounces Brie, cut into 4 slices
¼ cup dairy sour cream
2 tablespoons chopped green onion
1 medium-size red bell pepper, cut into ¼-inch rings
4 (2½-inch) slices Italian or French bread, halved
4 radicchio or lettuce leaves

Mix ground beef and 3 tablespoons steak sauce; shape into 8 thin patties. Place 1 slice Brie in center of each of 4 patties. Top with remaining patties. Seal edges to form 4 patties; set aside.

Blend sour cream, remaining 2 tablespoons steak sauce and green onion; set aside.

Grill burgers over medium heat or broil 6 inches from heat source 7 minutes on each side or until beef is no longer pink. Place pepper rings on grill or under broiler; cook with burgers until tender, about 4 to 5 minutes. Top each of 4 bread slice halves with radicchio leaf, pepper ring, burger, 2 tablespoons reserved sauce and another bread slice half. Serve immediately. Garnish as desired.   *Makes 4 servings*

Cajun Chicken Burgers

1 pound fresh ground chicken *or* turkey
1 small onion, finely chopped
¼ cup chopped bell pepper
3 scallions, minced
1 clove garlic, minced
1 teaspoon Worcestershire sauce
½ teaspoon TABASCO® brand Pepper Sauce
    Dash ground pepper

Combine all ingredients in medium bowl. Form into 4-inch patties. Broil or grill 4 to 6 minutes on each side or until cooked through. Serve immediately.   *Makes 5 servings*

Inside-Out Brie Burger

Easy Salmon Burgers with Honey Barbecue Sauce

⅓ cup honey
⅓ cup ketchup
1½ teaspoons cider vinegar
1 teaspoon prepared horseradish
¼ teaspoon minced garlic
⅛ teaspoon crushed red pepper flakes (optional)
1 can (7½ ounces) salmon, drained
½ cup dried bread crumbs
¼ cup chopped onion
3 tablespoons chopped green bell pepper
1 egg white
2 hamburger buns, toasted

In small bowl, combine honey, ketchup, vinegar, horseradish, garlic and red pepper flakes until well blended. Set aside half of sauce. In separate bowl, mix together salmon, bread crumbs, onion, green pepper and egg white. Blend in 2 tablespoons of sauce. Divide salmon mixture into 2 patties, ½ to ¾ inch thick. Place patties on well-oiled grill, 4 to 6 inches from hot coals. Grill, turning 2 to 3 times and basting with sauce, until burgers are browned and cooked through. Or place patties on lightly greased baking sheet. Broil 4 to 6 inches from heat source, turning 2 to 3 times and basting with sauce, until cooked through. Place on hamburger buns and serve with reserved sauce.

Makes 2 servings

Favorite recipe from **National Honey Board**

Cheddar-Stuffed Mesquite Burgers

½ cup LAWRY'S® Mesquite Marinade with Lime Juice
1 pound ground beef
½ cup chopped green bell pepper
½ cup finely chopped onion
¼ cup unseasoned bread crumbs
½ teaspoon LAWRY'S® Seasoned Pepper
½ cup (2 ounces) shredded cheddar cheese
4 hamburger buns, toasted
Lettuce leaves
Tomato slices

In large bowl, combine Mesquite Marinade, ground beef, bell pepper, onion, bread crumbs and Seasoned Pepper; mix well. Let stand 20 minutes. Shape meat into 8 thin patties. In center of 4 patties, place layer of cheese. Top with remaining patties. Press edges tightly together to seal. Grill or broil burgers 8 to 10 minutes or until desired doneness, turning halfway through grilling time. Serve burgers on toasted buns with lettuce and tomato. *Makes 4 servings*

Hint: Ground turkey is an excellent substitute for ground beef.

Burrito Turkey Burgers

    Vegetable cooking spray
2 pounds ground turkey
1 cup chopped onion
1 can (4 ounces) chopped green chilies, drained
1 package (1¼ ounces) taco seasoning mix
8 (8-inch) flour tortillas
1 can (16 ounces) nonfat refried beans
    Shredded lettuce
½ cup shredded nonfat Cheddar cheese, divided
    Salsa (optional)

1. Spray cold grill rack with vegetable cooking spray. Preheat charcoal grill for direct-heat cooking.

2. In medium bowl combine turkey, onion, chilies and seasoning mix. Shape turkey mixture into 8 (9×32-inch) rectangular-shaped burgers. Grill burgers 3 to 4 minutes; turn and continue cooking 2 to 3 minutes or until 160°F is reached on meat thermometer and meat is no longer pink in center. Remove and keep warm.

3. Heat tortillas according to package directions. Spread each tortilla with ¼ cup refried beans and sprinkle with lettuce. Place 1 burger in center of each tortilla and sprinkle with 1 tablespoon cheese. Fold sides of tortillas over burgers to create burritos. Serve with salsa, if desired.
Makes 8 servings

Favorite recipe from **National Turkey Federation**

Southwest Pesto Burgers

CILANTRO PESTO
  1 large clove garlic
  4 ounces fresh cilantro, stems removed and rinsed
  1½ teaspoons bottled minced jalapeño pepper *or* 1 tablespoon
      bottled sliced jalapeño pepper,* drained
  ¼ teaspoon salt
  ¼ cup vegetable oil

BURGERS
  1¼ pounds ground beef
  ¼ cup plus 1 tablespoon Cilantro Pesto, divided
  ½ teaspoon salt
  4 slices pepper jack cheese
  2 tablespoons light or regular mayonnaise
  4 Kaiser rolls, split
  1 ripe avocado, peeled and sliced
     Salsa

*Jalapeño peppers can sting and irritate the skin; wear rubber gloves when handling peppers and do not touch eyes. Wash hands after handling.

1. For pesto, with motor running, drop garlic through feed tube of food processor; process until minced. Add cilantro, jalapeño pepper and ¼ teaspoon salt; process until cilantro is chopped.

2. With motor running, slowly add oil through feed tube; process until thick paste forms. Transfer to container with tight-fitting lid. Store in refrigerator up to 3 weeks.

3. Prepare barbecue grill for direct cooking.

4. Combine beef, ¼ cup pesto and ½ teaspoon salt in large bowl; mix well. Form into 4 patties. Place patties on grid over medium-hot coals. Grill, uncovered, 4 to 5 minutes per side or until meat is no longer pink in center. Add cheese to patties during last 1 minute of grilling.

5. While patties are cooking, combine mayonnaise and remaining 1 tablespoon pesto in small bowl; mix well. Top patties with mayonnaise mixture. Serve on rolls with avocado and salsa.

Makes 4 servings

Serving Suggestion: Serve with refried beans.

Prep and Cook Time: 20 minutes

Southwest Pesto Burger

Mediterranean Burgers

½ cup feta cheese (2 ounces)
¼ cup A.1.® Original or A.1.® BOLD & SPICY Steak Sauce, divided
2 tablespoons sliced pitted ripe olives
2 tablespoons mayonnaise
1 pound ground beef
4 (5-inch) pita breads
4 radicchio leaves
4 tomato slices

Mix feta cheese, 2 tablespoons steak sauce, olives and mayonnaise. Cover; refrigerate at least one hour or up to 2 days.

Shape beef into 4 patties. Grill burgers over medium heat or broil 6 inches from heat source 5 minutes on each side or until no longer pink in center, basting with remaining 2 tablespoons steak sauce.

Split open top edge of each pita bread. Arrange 1 radicchio leaf in each pita pocket; top each with burger, tomato slice and 2 tablespoons chilled sauce. Serve immediately.

Bistro Burgers with Blue Cheese

1 pound ground turkey or beef
¼ cup chopped fresh parsley
2 tablespoons minced chives
2 tablespoons FRENCH'S® Dijon Mustard
¼ teaspoon dried thyme leaves
2 ounces blue cheese, cut into 4 squares
   (about 1½×¼ inch thick)
Lettuce and tomato slices
4 crusty rolls, split in half

1. Gently combine turkey, parsley, chives, mustard and thyme in large bowl. Divide meat evenly into 8 portions. Shape each into thin patty, about 3 inches in diameter. Place 1 piece cheese between 2 patties, firmly pressing edges together to seal.

2. Place patties on oiled grid. Grill over medium-high heat 15 minutes or until no longer pink. Arrange lettuce and tomatoes on bottom halves of rolls. Top with burgers and top halves of rolls. Serve with additional mustard, if desired.   *Makes 4 servings*

Prep Time: 15 minutes
Cook Time: 15 minutes

Mediterranean Burger

Just Kabobbing Along

Grilled Vegetable Kabobs

  1 large red or green bell pepper
  1 large zucchini
  1 large yellow squash or additional zucchini
 12 ounces large mushrooms
  2 tablespoons olive oil
  2 tablespoons red wine vinegar
  1 package (7.2 ounces) RICE-A-RONI® Herb & Butter
  1 large tomato, chopped
  ¼ cup grated Parmesan cheese

1. Cut red pepper into twelve 1-inch pieces. Cut zucchini and yellow squash crosswise into twelve ½-inch slices. Marinate red pepper, zucchini, yellow squash and mushrooms in combined oil and vinegar 15 minutes.

2. Alternately thread marinated vegetables onto 4 large metal skewers. Brush with any remaining oil mixture; set aside.

3. Prepare Rice-A-Roni® Mix as package directs.

4. While Rice-A-Roni® is simmering, grill kabobs over medium-low coals or broil 4 to 5 inches from heat 12 to 14 minutes or until tender and browned, turning once.

5. Stir tomato into rice. Serve rice topped with kabobs. Sprinkle with cheese.   *Makes 4 servings*

Apple-icious Lamb Kabobs

    1 cup apple juice or cider
    2 tablespoons Worcestershire sauce
    ½ teaspoon lemon pepper
    2 cloves garlic, peeled and sliced
 1½ pounds fresh American lamb (leg or shoulder), cut into
        1¼-inch cubes
    Apple Barbecue Sauce (recipe follows)
    1 large apple, cut into 12 wedges
    Assorted vegetables, such as green or red bell pepper, onion or
        summer squash, cut into wedges

Combine apple juice, Worcestershire sauce, lemon pepper and garlic in large resealable plastic food storage bag or nonmetal container. Add lamb cubes and coat well. To marinate, refrigerate 2 to 24 hours.

Prepare Apple Barbecue Sauce. Preheat grill or broiler. Remove meat from marinade and thread onto skewers, alternating meat, apple and vegetables. (If using bamboo skewers, soak in water for 20 to 30 minutes before using to prevent them from burning.)

To grill, place kabobs 4 inches from medium coals. Cook about 10 to 12 minutes, turning occasionally and brushing with Apple Barbecue Sauce. To broil, place kabobs on broiler pan sprayed with nonstick cooking spray. Broil 4 inches from heat about 10 to 12 minutes for medium-rare, turning occasionally and brushing with Apple Barbecue Sauce.   *Makes 6 servings*

Apple Barbecue Sauce

    ½ cup apple juice or cider
    ½ cup finely chopped onion
    1 cup chili sauce
    ½ cup unsweetened applesauce
    2 tablespoons packed brown sugar
    1 tablespoon Worcestershire sauce
    1 teaspoon dry mustard
    5 drops hot pepper sauce

Combine apple juice and onion in small saucepan; simmer 2 minutes. Stir in chili sauce, applesauce, brown sugar, Worcestershire sauce, dry mustard and hot pepper sauce. Simmer 10 minutes, stirring occasionally. Remove from heat.

Favorite recipe from **American Lamb Council**

Apple-icious Lamb Kabob

Sun-Kissed Shrimp Kabobs

16 jumbo-size shrimp (about 1 pound)
⅓ cup KIKKOMAN® Teriyaki Marinade & Sauce
1 green onion and tops, minced
1 clove garlic, pressed
1 teaspoon grated lemon peel
½ teaspoon sugar
1 can (8 ounces) pineapple chunks in syrup, drained

Leaving shells on tails, peel shrimp; devein. Combine teriyaki sauce, green onion, garlic, lemon peel and sugar in medium bowl. Add shrimp; toss to coat well. Reserving teriyaki sauce mixture, remove shrimp and place 1 pineapple chunk in curve of each shrimp. Thread each of 4 (12-inch) metal or bamboo* skewers with 4 shrimp and pineapple. Place kabobs on grill 4 to 5 inches from hot coals; brush with reserved teriyaki sauce mixture. Cook 4 minutes; turn kabobs over. Brush with remaining teriyaki sauce mixture. Cook 3 minutes longer, or just until shrimp turn pink. (Or, place kabobs on rack of broiler pan 4 to 5 inches from heat. Brush with reserved teriyaki sauce mixture. Broil 4 minutes; turn over. Brush with remaining teriyaki sauce mixture. Broil 4 minutes longer, or until shrimp turn pink.)   *Makes 4 servings*

*Soak bamboo skewers in water 30 minutes to prevent burning.

Hickory Beef Kabobs

1 pound boneless beef top sirloin or tenderloin steak, cut into
    1¼-inch pieces
2 ears fresh corn,* shucked, cleaned and cut crosswise into
    1-inch pieces
1 red or green bell pepper, cut into 1-inch squares
1 small red onion, cut into ½-inch wedges
½ cup beer
½ cup chili sauce
1 teaspoon dry mustard
2 cloves garlic, minced
3 cups hot cooked white rice
¼ cup chopped fresh parsley

*Four small ears frozen corn, thawed, can be substituted for fresh corn.

1. Place beef, corn, bell pepper and onion in large resealable plastic food storage bag. Combine beer, chili sauce, mustard and garlic in small bowl; pour over beef and vegetables. Seal bag tightly, turning to coat. Marinate in refrigerator at least 1 hour or up to 8 hours, turning occasionally.

2. Prepare grill for direct cooking. Meanwhile, cover 1½ cups hickory chips with cold water; soak 20 minutes.

3. Drain beef and vegetables; reserve marinade. Alternately thread beef and vegetables onto 4 (12-inch) metal skewers. Brush with reserved marinade.

4. Drain hickory chips; sprinkle over coals. Place kabobs on grid. Grill kabobs on covered grill, over medium-hot coals, 5 minutes. Brush with reserved marinade; turn and brush again. Discard remaining marinade. Continue to grill, covered, 5 to 7 minutes for medium or until desired doneness is reached.

5. Combine rice and chopped parsley; serve kabobs over rice mixture.
Makes 4 servings

Caribbean Pork Kabobs and Rice

1 cup UNCLE BEN'S® CONVERTED® Brand Original Rice
1½ cups peeled, diced sweet potato
2 tablespoons plus 2 teaspoons Caribbean seasoning, divided
1 can (8 ounces) pineapple chunks in pineapple juice
1 (12-ounce) pork tenderloin, cut into 1½-inch cubes
1 red bell pepper, cut into 1-inch squares
1 green bell pepper, cut into 1-inch squares
¼ cup dry-roasted peanuts

1. In medium pan, heat 2 cups water to a boil. Add rice, sweet potato and 2 teaspoons Caribbean seasoning. Cover, reduce heat and simmer 10 minutes or until rice and sweet potato are tender.

2. Drain pineapple chunks, reserving juice. Add pineapple chunks to rice mixture.

3. Preheat broiler. Place remaining 2 tablespoons Caribbean seasoning into large resealable plastic food storage bag. Add pork; seal bag and turn to coat pork with seasoning. Thread pork and bell peppers onto skewers.

4. Broil kabobs 4 minutes on each side. Turn and brush with reserved pineapple juice. Continue cooking 2 minutes on each side until pork is no longer pink.

5. Top rice with peanuts and serve with kabobs. *Makes 4 servings*

Caribbean Pork Kabobs and Rice

Cowboy Kabobs

½ cup A.1.® Original or A.1.® BOLD & SPICY Steak Sauce
½ cup barbecue sauce
2½ teaspoons prepared horseradish
1 (1½-pound) beef top round steak, cut into ½-inch strips
4 medium-size red skin potatoes, cut into wedges, blanched
1 medium onion, cut into wedges
⅓ cup red bell pepper strips
⅓ cup green bell pepper strips
⅓ cup yellow bell pepper strips

Soak 8 (10-inch) wooden skewers in water at least 30 minutes.

Blend steak sauce, barbecue sauce and horseradish; set aside.

Alternately thread steak strips (accordion-style) and vegetables onto skewers. Place kabobs in nonmetal dish; coat with ⅔ cup reserved steak sauce mixture. Cover; refrigerate 1 hour, turning occasionally.

Remove kabobs from marinade; discard marinade. Grill kabobs over medium heat or broil 6 inches from heat source 6 to 10 minutes or until steak is desired doneness, turning occasionally and basting with remaining steak sauce mixture. Serve immediately.

Makes 4 servings

BBQ Beer Brat Kabobs

1 package BOB EVANS® Beer Bratwurst (approximately 5 links), cut into 1-inch pieces
1 medium zucchini, cut into 1-inch pieces
1 medium yellow squash, cut into 1-inch pieces
1 medium red onion, cut into 1-inch pieces
1 green bell pepper, cut into 1-inch pieces
1 red bell pepper, cut into 1-inch pieces
2 cups fresh button mushroom caps
2 cups BOB EVANS® Barbecue Sauce

Soak 6 (10-inch) wooden skewers in water 30 minutes. Alternately thread bratwurst and vegetables onto skewers. Grill or broil kabobs 12 to 15 minutes or until brats are cooked through, turning and brushing occasionally with barbecue sauce. Refrigerate leftovers.

Makes 6 kabobs

Cowboy Kabobs

Tex-Mex Pork Kabobs with Chili Sour Cream Sauce

2¼ teaspoons chili powder, divided
1¾ teaspoons cumin, divided
¾ teaspoon garlic powder, divided
¾ teaspoon onion powder, divided
¾ teaspoon oregano, divided
1 pork tenderloin (1½ pounds), trimmed and cut into 1-inch pieces
1 cup reduced-fat sour cream
¾ teaspoon salt, divided
¼ teaspoon black pepper
1 large red bell pepper, cored, seeded and cut into small chunks
1 large green bell pepper, cored, seeded and cut into small chunks
1 large yellow bell pepper, cored, seeded and cut into small chunks

Blend 1½ teaspoons chili powder, 1 teaspoon cumin, ½ teaspoon garlic powder, ½ teaspoon onion powder and ½ teaspoon oregano in medium bowl. Add pork. Toss well to coat. Cover tightly and refrigerate 2 to 3 hours.

Combine sour cream, remaining spices, ¼ teaspoon salt and pepper in small bowl. Mix well. Cover tightly and refrigerate 2 to 3 hours.

If using wooden skewers, soak in water 20 minutes before using. Prepare grill for direct cooking.

Toss pork with remaining ½ teaspoon salt. Thread meat and peppers onto skewers. Grill over medium-hot coals 10 minutes or until meat is no longer pink in center, turning several times. Serve immediately with sour cream sauce. *Makes 4 to 6 servings*

Italian Chicken Kabobs

½ cup Italian salad dressing
¼ cup chopped fresh basil leaves
1 medium yellow onion, peeled
1 medium red bell pepper, seeded
1 medium zucchini, scrubbed
1 small jicama, peeled
1 package (about 1 pound) PERDUE® Fresh Italian Seasoned
    Boneless Chicken Breasts

In large bowl, combine Italian dressing with basil. Cut vegetables into chunks; place in dressing. Cover and marinate 1 to 2 hours.

Prepare grill for cooking. Cut chicken into 1½-inch chunks. On metal skewers, thread chicken chunks, alternating with marinated vegetables, until all ingredients are used. Grill kabobs over medium-hot coals 10 to 15 minutes, until chicken is cooked through, turning occasionally.

Makes 4 servings

Glazed Frank Kabobs

1 package (16 ounces) HEBREW NATIONAL® Quarter Pound
    Dinner Beef Franks, cut into 16 (1½-inch) pieces
1 small red onion, peeled, cut into ½-inch wedges
1 red bell pepper, seeded, cut into 1-inch pieces
1 green bell pepper, seeded, cut into 1-inch pieces
2 ears fresh corn, shucked or 4 small ears frozen corn on the
    cob, thawed, cut crosswise into 1-inch slices
½ cup chili sauce
3 tablespoons light brown sugar
2 tablespoons HEBREW NATIONAL® Deli Mustard

Prepare barbecue grill for direct cooking. Alternately thread franks and vegetables onto metal skewers. Set aside.

Combine chili sauce, sugar and mustard in small bowl; mix well. Place kabobs on grid over medium-hot coals. Brush with half of sauce. Grill, on covered grill, 5 minutes. Turn kabobs; brush with remaining sauce. Grill, covered, 5 to 7 minutes or until vegetables and franks are tender.

Makes 4 servings

Chicken Teriyaki Kabobs

4 boneless, skinless chicken breast halves (about 1 pound), cut
   into 1-inch cubes
2 medium zucchini, cut into ½-inch-thick slices
1 medium-sized green bell pepper, cut into 1-inch squares
1 small red onion, cut into ½-inch cubes
1 cup LAWRY'S® Teriyaki Marinade with Pineapple Juice, divided
½ teaspoon LAWRY'S® Seasoned Pepper
¼ teaspoon LAWRY'S® Garlic Powder with Parsley

Place chicken and vegetables on skewers, alternating chicken with
vegetables. Place in large shallow baking dish. Pour ¾ cup Teriyaki
Marinade with Pineapple Juice over kabobs. Turn kabobs over to coat all
sides. Cover dish. Refrigerate at least 30 minutes, turning once. Remove
skewers from marinade; discard marinade. Sprinkle skewers with
Seasoned Pepper and Garlic Powder with Parsley. Grill or broil skewers
10 to 15 minutes or until chicken is no longer pink in center and juices
run clear when cut, turning and basting often with remaining ¼ cup
Teriyaki Marinade with Pineapple Juice. *Do not baste during last
5 minutes of cooking.*   *Makes 6 servings*

Serving Suggestion: Great served with steamed rice or baked potatoes.

Cilantro-Lime Chicken and Mango Kabobs

1 pound boneless skinless chicken breasts, cut into thin strips
1 large mango, peeled and cut into chunks
1 large green pepper, cut into 1-inch squares
3 tablespoons honey
3 tablespoons lime juice
1 teaspoon grated lime peel
2 tablespoons FLEISCHMANN'S® Original Margarine
2 tablespoons chopped cilantro or parsley

Thread chicken, mango and pepper alternately on 8 skewers; set aside.

In small saucepan, over medium heat, heat honey, lime juice, lime peel,
margarine and cilantro until hot. Keep warm.

Broil or grill kabobs 4 inches from heat 12 to 15 minutes or until
chicken is cooked, turning and brushing with honey mixture often.
Reheat any remaining honey mixture to a boil; serve with kabobs.
                          Makes 8 appetizers or 4 main-dish servings

Chicken Teriyaki Kabobs

Crazy for Chicken

Orange-Mint Chicken

1 broiler-fryer chicken (2½ to 3 pounds), cut into halves
2 teaspoons LAWRY'S® Seasoned Salt
½ cup orange marmalade
3 tablespoons butter
3 tablespoons honey
1 teaspoon crushed dried mint leaves
Wedged orange (garnish)
Fresh mint leaves (garnish)

Sprinkle Seasoned Salt over chicken. Let stand 10 to 15 minutes. In medium saucepan, combine marmalade, butter, honey and mint. Heat 1 to 2 minutes, stirring frequently. Grill or broil chicken 35 to 45 minutes or until no longer pink in center and juices run clear when cut, turning once and basting often with marmalade mixture. *Do not baste during last 5 minutes of cooking.* Discard any remaining marmalade mixture.

Makes 4 to 6 servings

Serving Suggestion: Serve with wild rice pilaf and garnish with orange wedges and fresh mint, if desired.

Buffalo Chicken Drumsticks

       8 large chicken drumsticks (about 2 pounds)
       3 tablespoons hot pepper sauce
       1 tablespoon vegetable oil
       1 clove garlic, minced
    ¼ cup mayonnaise
       3 tablespoons sour cream
    1½ tablespoons white wine vinegar
    ¼ teaspoon sugar
    ⅓ cup (1½ ounces) crumbled Roquefort or blue cheese
       2 cups hickory chips
         Celery sticks

Place chicken in large resealable plastic food storage bag. Combine
pepper sauce, oil and garlic in small bowl; pour over chicken. Seal bag
tightly; turn to coat. Marinate in refrigerator at least 1 hour or, for
hotter flavor, up to 24 hours, turning occasionally.

For blue cheese dressing, combine mayonnaise, sour cream, vinegar
and sugar in another small bowl. Stir in cheese; cover and refrigerate
until serving.

Prepare grill. Meanwhile, cover hickory chips with cold water; soak
20 minutes. Drain chicken, discarding marinade. Drain hickory chips;
sprinkle over coals. Place chicken on grid. Grill on covered grill, over
medium-hot coals, 25 to 30 minutes or until chicken is tender when
pierced with fork and no longer pink near bone, turning 3 to 4 times.
Serve with blue cheese dressing and celery sticks.   *Makes 4 servings*

Buffalo Chicken Drumsticks

Grilled Chicken Fajitas

3 boneless skinless chicken breast halves (about ¾ pound)
1 clove garlic, halved
1 medium green or red pepper, quartered
½ red onion, sliced ¼ inch thick
1½ cups VELVEETA® Shredded Pasteurized Process Cheese Food
6 flour tortillas (6 inch), warmed
TACO BELL® HOME ORIGINALS®* Thick 'N Chunky Salsa

*TACO BELL and HOME ORIGINALS are registered trademarks owned and licensed by Taco Bell Corp.

1. Rub both sides of chicken with garlic. Place chicken, green pepper and onion slices on greased grill over medium-hot coals.

2. Grill 20 minutes or until cooked through, turning occasionally. Cut chicken and green pepper into thin strips.

3. Spoon chicken mixture and ¼ cup Velveeta in center of each tortilla; fold. Serve with salsa.   *Makes 6 servings*

Use Your Stove: Cut chicken into strips. Spray skillet with no stick cooking spray. Add chicken and 1 clove garlic, minced; cook and stir on medium-high heat 5 minutes. Add green pepper, cut into strips, and onion; cook and stir 4 to 5 minutes or until chicken is cooked through and vegetables are tender-crisp. Continue as directed.

Prep Time: 10 minutes
Grill Time: 20 minutes

Grilled Chicken Fajita

Chicken Teriyaki

8 large chicken drumsticks (about 2 pounds)
⅓ cup teriyaki sauce
2 tablespoons brandy or apple juice
1 green onion, minced
1 tablespoon vegetable oil
1 teaspoon ground ginger
½ teaspoon sugar
¼ teaspoon garlic powder
   Prepared sweet-and-sour sauce (optional)

Place chicken in large resealable plastic food storage bag. Combine teriyaki sauce, brandy, onion, oil, ginger, sugar and garlic powder in small bowl; pour over chicken. Close bag securely, turning to coat. Marinate in refrigerator at least 1 hour or overnight, turning occasionally.

Prepare grill for indirect cooking.

Drain chicken; reserve marinade. Place chicken on grid directly over drip pan. Grill, covered, over medium-high heat 60 minutes or until chicken is no longer pink in center and juices run clear, turning and brushing with reserved marinade every 20 minutes. Do not brush with marinade during last 5 minutes of grilling; discard remaining marinade. Serve with sweet-and-sour sauce, if desired.   *Makes 4 servings*

Spicy Island Chicken

   1 cup finely chopped white onion
   ⅓ cup white wine vinegar
   6 green onions, finely chopped
   6 cloves garlic, minced
   1 habañero or serrano pepper,* finely chopped
4½ teaspoons olive oil
4½ teaspoons fresh thyme leaves *or* 2 teaspoons dried thyme
        leaves
   1 tablespoon ground allspice
   2 teaspoons sugar
   1 teaspoon salt
   1 teaspoon ground cinnamon
   1 teaspoon ground nutmeg
   1 teaspoon black pepper
   ½ teaspoon ground red pepper
   6 boneless skinless chicken breasts

*Habañero peppers can sting and irritate the skin; wear rubber gloves when handling peppers and do not touch eyes. Wash hands after handling.

1. Combine all ingredients except chicken in medium bowl; mix well. Place chicken in resealable plastic food storage bag and add seasoning mixture. Seal bag; turn to coat chicken. Marinate in refrigerator 4 hours or overnight.

2. Spray cold grid with nonstick cooking spray. Adjust grid to 4 to 6 inches above heat. Preheat grill to medium-high heat.

3. Remove chicken from marinade. Reserve marinade. Grill 5 to 7 minutes per side or until chicken is no longer pink in center, brushing occasionally with marinade. *Do not brush with marinade during last 5 minutes of grilling.* Discard remaining marinade.   *Makes 6 servings*

Hot 'n' Spicy Chicken Barbecue

½ cup A.1.® Steak Sauce
½ cup tomato sauce
¼ cup finely chopped onion
2 tablespoons cider vinegar
2 tablespoons maple syrup
1 tablespoon vegetable oil
2 teaspoons chili powder
½ teaspoon crushed red pepper flakes
1 (3-pound) chicken, cut up

Blend steak sauce, tomato sauce, onion, vinegar, maple syrup, oil, chili powder and red pepper flakes in medium saucepan. Heat mixture to a boil over medium heat; reduce heat. Simmer for 5 to 7 minutes or until thickened; cool.

Grill chicken over medium heat for 30 to 40 minutes or until done, turning and basting frequently with prepared sauce. Serve hot.

Makes 4 servings

Tequila Sunrise Chicken

4 boneless, skinless chicken breasts
⅓ cup lime juice
2 tablespoons KNOTT'S® Jalapeño Jelly
2 tablespoons chopped fresh cilantro
2 tablespoons tequila
2 tablespoons olive oil
1 teaspoon minced fresh garlic
¼ teaspoon salt
¼ teaspoon pepper

1. Rinse and pat dry chicken. Arrange chicken in 8×8×2-inch baking dish; set aside.

2. In small bowl, combine *remaining* ingredients. Pour half the marinade over chicken and reserve *remaining* marinade for basting. Refrigerate chicken 2 to 8 hours.

3. Place chicken on grill over hot coals. Grill chicken until no longer pink and juices run clear, basting frequently with reserved marinade.

Makes 4 servings

Hot 'n' Spicy Chicken Barbecue

Jamaican Rum Chicken

½ cup dark rum
2 tablespoons lime juice or lemon juice
2 tablespoons soy sauce
2 tablespoons brown sugar
4 large cloves garlic, minced
1 to 2 jalapeño peppers,* seeded and minced
1 tablespoon minced fresh ginger
1 teaspoon dried thyme leaves, crushed
½ teaspoon black pepper
6 boneless skinless chicken breast halves

*Jalapeño peppers can sting and irritate the skin; wear rubber gloves when handling peppers and do not touch eyes. Wash hands after handling.

1. To prepare marinade, combine rum, lime juice, soy sauce, sugar, garlic, jalapeño peppers, ginger, thyme and black pepper in 2-quart glass measuring cup.

2. Rinse chicken and pat dry with paper towels. Place chicken in resealable plastic food storage bag. Pour marinade over chicken. Press air out of bag and seal tightly. Turn bag over to completely coat chicken with marinade. Refrigerate 4 hours or overnight, turning bag once or twice.

3. Prepare barbecue grill for direct grilling by spreading hot coals in single layer that extends 1 to 2 inches beyond area of food.

4. Drain chicken; reserve marinade. Place chicken on grid. Grill chicken on uncovered grill, over medium-hot coals, 6 minutes per side or until chicken is no longer pink in center.

5. Meanwhile, bring remaining marinade to a boil in small saucepan over medium-high heat. Boil 5 minutes or until marinade is reduced by about half.

6. To serve, drizzle marinade over chicken. Garnish as desired.

Makes 6 servings

Jamaican Rum Chicken

Carolina-Style Barbecue Chicken

 2 pounds boneless skinless chicken breast halves or thighs
¾ cup packed light brown sugar, divided
¾ cup FRENCH'S® Classic Yellow® Mustard
½ cup cider vinegar
¼ cup *Frank's® RedHot® Sauce*
 2 tablespoons vegetable oil
 2 tablespoons FRENCH'S® Worcestershire Sauce
½ teaspoon salt
¼ teaspoon black pepper

1. Place chicken in large resealable plastic food storage bag. Combine ½ cup brown sugar, mustard, vinegar, **RedHot** Sauce, oil, Worcestershire, salt and pepper in 4-cup measure; mix well. Pour 1 cup mustard mixture over chicken. Seal bag; marinate in refrigerator 1 hour or overnight.

2. Pour remaining mustard mixture into small saucepan. Stir in remaining ¼ cup sugar. Bring to a boil. Reduce heat; simmer 5 minutes or until sugar dissolves and mixture thickens slightly, stirring often. Reserve for serving sauce.

3. Place chicken on well-oiled grid, reserving marinade. Grill over high heat 10 to 15 minutes or until chicken is no longer pink in center, turning and basting once with marinade. *Do not baste during last 5 minutes of cooking.* Discard any remaining marinade. Serve chicken with reserved sauce. *Makes 8 servings*

Prep Time: 15 minutes
Marinate Time: 1 hour
Cook Time: 10 minutes

Carolina-Style Barbecue Chicken

Grilled Chicken & Fresh Salsa Wraps

1 bottle (12 ounces) LAWRY'S® Herb & Garlic Marinade with Lemon Juice, divided
4 boneless, skinless chicken breast halves (about 1 pound)
1 large tomato, chopped
1 can (4 ounces) diced mild green chiles, drained (optional)
¼ cup thinly sliced green onions
1 tablespoon red wine vinegar
1 tablespoon chopped fresh cilantro
½ teaspoon LAWRY'S® Garlic Salt
4 to 8 flour tortillas, warmed

In large resealable plastic food storage bag, combine 1 cup Herb & Garlic Marinade and chicken; seal bag. Marinate in refrigerator at least 30 minutes. In medium bowl, combine tomato, chiles, if desired, green onions, additional ¼ cup Herb & Garlic Marinade, vinegar, cilantro and Garlic Salt; mix well. Cover and refrigerate 30 minutes or until chilled. Remove chicken; discard used marinade. Grill or broil chicken 10 to 15 minutes or until no longer pink in center and juices run clear when cut, turning halfway through grilling time. Cut chicken into strips. Place chicken on tortillas; spoon salsa on top and wrap to enclose. Serve immediately. *Makes 4 servings*

Serving Suggestion: Serve with black bean and corn salad.

Hint: This is an excellent recipe for picnics or outdoor dining. Assemble wraps when ready to serve.

Barbecued Chicken with Chili-Orange Glaze

1 to 2 dried de arbol chilies*
½ cup fresh orange juice
2 tablespoons tequila
1½ teaspoons shredded orange peel
2 cloves garlic, minced
¼ teaspoon salt
¼ cup vegetable oil
1 whole chicken (about 3 pounds), cut into quarters
Orange slices (optional)
Cilantro sprigs (optional)

*For milder flavor, discard seeds from chili peppers. Since chili peppers can sting and irritate the skin, wear rubber gloves when handling peppers and do not touch eyes. Wash your hands after handling chili peppers.

Crush chilies into coarse flakes. Combine chilies, orange juice, tequila, orange peel, garlic and salt in small bowl. Gradually add oil, whisking continuously until marinade is thoroughly blended.

Arrange chicken in single layer in shallow glass baking dish. Pour marinade over chicken; turn pieces to coat. Marinate, covered, in refrigerator 2 to 3 hours, turning chicken over and basting with marinade several times.

Prepare charcoal grill for direct cooking. Drain chicken, reserving marinade. Bring marinade to a boil in small saucepan over high heat. Grill chicken on covered grill 6 to 8 inches from heat 15 minutes, brushing frequently with marinade. Turn chicken over. Grill 15 minutes more or until chicken is no longer pink in center and juices run clear, brushing frequently with marinade. *Do not baste during last 5 minutes of grilling.* Garnish with orange slices and cilantro, if desired.

Makes 4 servings

Hot and Spicy Pick of the Chick

   1 jar (5 ounces) roasted peppers, drained
   1 can (4 ounces) mild green chilies, drained
   2 tablespoons brown sugar
   2 tablespoons canola oil
   2 tablespoons lime juice
1½ teaspoons hot pepper sauce
   1 teaspoon ground cumin
   1 teaspoon salt
   2 to 3 sprigs fresh cilantro
   1 package (about 4 pounds) PERDUE® Fresh Pick of the Chicken

Prepare lightly greased grill for cooking. In food processor or blender, combine all ingredients except chicken; puree until smooth. Set aside ½ cup sauce.

Grill chicken, uncovered, 5 to 6 inches over medium-hot coals about 30 minutes or until cooked through, turning and basting with sauce 3 to 4 times during grilling. Serve reserved ½ cup sauce as a condiment with grilled chicken.

Makes about 6 to 8 servings

Meaty Main Courses

Jamaican Baby Back Ribs

2 tablespoons sugar
2 tablespoons fresh lemon juice
1 tablespoon salt
1 tablespoon vegetable oil
2 teaspoons black pepper
2 teaspoons dried thyme leaves, crushed
¾ teaspoon *each* ground cinnamon, nutmeg and allspice
½ teaspoon ground red pepper
6 pounds well-trimmed pork baby back ribs, cut into
   3- to 4-rib portions
Barbecue Sauce (page 210)

1. For seasoning rub, combine all ingredients except ribs and Barbecue Sauce in small bowl; stir well. Spread over all surfaces of ribs; press with fingertips so mixture adheres to ribs. Cover; refrigerate overnight.

2. Prepare grill for indirect cooking. While coals are heating, prepare barbecue sauce.

3. Place seasoned ribs directly on cooking grid directly over drip pan. Grill, covered, 1 hour, turning occasionally.

4. Baste ribs generously with Barbecue Sauce; grill 30 minutes more or until ribs are tender and browned, turning occasionally.

5. Bring remaining Barbecue Sauce to a boil over medium-high heat; boil 1 minute. Serve ribs with remaining sauce.

Makes 6 servings
continued on page 210

Jamaican Baby Back ribs, continued

Barbecue Sauce

  2 tablespoons butter
½ cup finely chopped onion
1½ cups ketchup
  1 cup red currant jelly
¼ cup apple cider vinegar
  1 tablespoon soy sauce
¼ teaspoon *each* ground red and black pepper

Melt butter in medium saucepan over medium-high heat. Add onion;
cook and stir until softened. Stir in remaining ingredients. Reduce heat
to medium-low; simmer 20 minutes, stirring often.

Makes about 3 cups

Grilled Apple-Stuffed Pork Chops

5 tablespoons FRENCH'S® Hearty Deli Brown Mustard, divided
3 tablespoons honey, divided
1 cup corn bread stuffing mix
1 small McIntosh apple, peeled, cored and chopped
¼ cup minced onion
¼ cup chopped fresh parsley
4 rib pork chops, cut 1¼ inches thick (about 2 pounds)

1. Combine ¼ cup water, 2 tablespoons mustard and 1 tablespoon
honey in medium bowl. Add stuffing mix, apple, onion and parsley;
toss until crumbs are moistened. Combine remaining 3 tablespoons
mustard and 2 tablespoons honey in small bowl; set aside for glaze.

2. Cut horizontal slits in pork chops, using sharp knife, to make pockets
for stuffing. Spoon stuffing evenly into pockets. Secure openings with
toothpicks.

3. Place pork chops on oiled grid. Grill over medium heat 40 to
45 minutes until no longer pink near bone, turning often. Baste chops
with reserved glaze during last 10 minutes of cooking.

Makes 4 servings

Prep Time: 20 minutes
Cook Time: 40 minutes

Szechuan Grilled Flank Steak

1 beef flank steak (1¼ to 1½ pounds)
¼ cup seasoned rice wine vinegar
¼ cup soy sauce
2 tablespoons dark sesame oil
4 cloves garlic, minced
2 teaspoons minced fresh ginger
½ teaspoon red pepper flakes
¼ cup water
½ cup thinly sliced green onions
2 to 3 teaspoons sesame seeds, toasted
Hot cooked rice (optional)

Place steak in large resealable plastic food storage bag. To prepare marinade, combine vinegar, soy sauce, oil, garlic, ginger and red pepper in small bowl; pour over steak. Press air from bag and seal; turn to coat. Marinate in refrigerator 3 hours, turning once.

Spray grid with nonstick cooking spray. Prepare coals for grilling. Drain steak, reserving marinade in small saucepan. Place steak on grid; grill, covered, over medium-hot coals 14 to 18 minutes for medium or to desired doneness, turning steak halfway through grilling time.

Add water to reserved marinade. Bring to a boil over high heat. Reduce heat to low; simmer 5 minutes. Transfer steak to carving board. Slice steak across grain into thin slices. Drizzle steak with boiled marinade. Sprinkle with green onions and sesame seeds. Serve with rice, if desired.

Makes 4 to 6 servings

Grilled Caribbean Steak with Tropical Fruit Rice

1 (1½-pound) flank steak
¼ cup soy sauce
1¼ cups orange juice, divided
1 teaspoon ground ginger
1 can (8 ounces) pineapple chunks in juice
¼ teaspoon ground allspice
1 cup UNCLE BEN'S® CONVERTED® Brand Original Rice
1 can (11 ounces) mandarin orange segments, drained

1. Place steak in large resealable plastic food storage bag. In small bowl, combine soy sauce, ¼ cup orange juice and ginger; pour over steak. Seal bag, turning to coat steak with marinade. Refrigerate steak, turning bag occasionally, at least 8 or up to 24 hours.

2. Drain pineapple, reserving juice. Combine remaining 1 cup orange juice and pineapple juice in 1-quart glass measure; add enough water to make 2¼ cups liquid.

3. In medium saucepan, combine juice mixture, allspice and salt to taste. Bring to a boil; stir in rice. Cover; reduce heat to low and simmer 20 minutes. Remove from heat and let stand, covered, 5 minutes.

4. Meanwhile, remove steak from marinade; discard marinade. Grill steak 7 minutes on each side for medium or until desired doneness. Cut steak diagonally across the grain into thin slices.

5. Place rice in serving bowl. Stir in pineapple and oranges. Serve with steak.

Makes 6 servings

Serving Suggestion: For an authentic Caribbean touch, add 1 cup diced peeled mango to rice with pineapple chunks and oranges.

Grilled Caribbean Steak with Tropical Fruit Rice

Herb and Orange Pork Chops

  2 cups orange juice
  3 tablespoons vegetable oil, divided
1½ teaspoons LAWRY'S® Seasoned Salt
1½ teaspoons LAWRY'S® Lemon Pepper
1½ teaspoons LAWRY'S® Garlic Powder with Parsley
  1 teaspoon dried basil, crushed
  ½ teaspoon dried rosemary, crushed
  4 pork loin chops, cut ½ inch thick
  ½ cup thinly sliced green onions
  1 teaspoon grated fresh orange peel

In large resealable plastic food storage bag combine orange juice,
2 tablespoons oil and next 5 ingredients; mix well. Remove 1 cup
marinade for basting. Add chops; seal bag. Marinate in refrigerator at
least 1 hour. Remove chops; discard used marinade. Grill or broil chops
8 to 10 minutes or until no longer pink in center, turning halfway
through grilling time. In large skillet, heat 1 tablespoon oil; add onions
and orange peel and cook over medium heat 1 minute. Add additional
marinade; reduce heat to low and cook until reduced by half. Serve
over chops. *Makes 4 servings*

Serving Suggestion: Serve with fresh fruit.

Grilled Jerk Steak

  4 teaspoons TABASCO® brand Pepper Sauce
  2 teaspoons salt
  1 teaspoon garlic powder
  1 teaspoon dried thyme leaves
  ¼ teaspoon ground allspice
  2 pounds boneless beef top loin steak

Combine all ingredients except steak in small bowl. Rub mixture on
both sides of steak. Cover and refrigerate at least 1 hour or overnight.
Bring to room temperature before grilling. Preheat grill or broiler. Place
steak on rack in grill or broiler pan. Grill steak 10 to 12 minutes for
medium-rare or until desired doneness, turning once.

Makes 4 servings

Herb and Orange Pork Chops

Peppered Steak with Dijon Sauce

4 boneless beef top loin or New York strip steaks, cut 1 inch thick (about 1½ pounds)
1 tablespoon FRENCH'S® Worcestershire Sauce
Crushed black pepper
⅓ cup mayonnaise
⅓ cup FRENCH'S® Dijon Mustard
3 tablespoons dry red wine
2 tablespoons minced red or green onion
2 tablespoons minced fresh parsley
1 clove garlic, minced

1. Brush steaks with Worcestershire and sprinkle with pepper to taste; set aside. To prepare Dijon sauce, combine mayonnaise, mustard, wine, onion, parsley and garlic in medium bowl.

2. Place steaks on grid. Grill steaks over high heat 15 minutes for medium rare or to desired doneness, turning often. Serve with Dijon sauce. *Makes 4 servings*

Tip: Dijon sauce is also great served with grilled salmon and swordfish. To serve with fish, substitute white wine for red wine and minced dill for fresh parsley.

Prep Time: 10 minutes
Cook Time: 15 minutes

Maple-Mustard-Glazed Spareribs

4 pounds pork spareribs
½ teaspoon salt
½ teaspoon pickling spices*
2 teaspoons vegetable oil
1 small onion, coarsely chopped
½ cup maple-flavored syrup
¼ cup cider vinegar
2 tablespoons water
1 tablespoon Dijon mustard
Dash salt
¼ teaspoon black pepper

*Pickling spices is a blend of seasonings used for pickling foods. It can include allspice, bay leaves, cardamom, coriander, cinnamon, cloves, ginger, mustard seeds and/or pepper. Most supermarkets carry prepackaged pickling spices in the spice aisle.

Sprinkle spareribs with ½ teaspoon salt. Place pickling spices in several thicknesses of cheesecloth; tie up to make a bouquet garni. Set aside. For glaze, heat oil in small saucepan; add onion. Cook and stir until tender. Add bouquet garni. Stir in syrup, vinegar, water, mustard, dash salt and pepper. Bring to a boil over medium-high heat; reduce heat to low and simmer 20 minutes. Discard bouquet garni.

Prepare grill with rectangular foil drip pan. Bank briquets on either side of drip pan for indirect cooking. Place ribs on grid over drip pan. Grill, on covered grill, over low coals 1½ hours or until ribs are tender, turning and basting occasionally with glaze. (Do not baste during last 5 minutes of grilling.) *Makes 4 servings*

Prep Time: 20 minutes
Cooking Time: 90 minutes

Favorite recipe from **National Pork Producers Council**

Lamb Chops with Cranberry-Orange Salsa

    1 medium orange, sectioned and chopped or ½ cup canned
        mandarin oranges, chopped
 ¼ cup finely chopped onion
 ¼ cup chopped green chilies, drained
 ¼ cup dried cranberries
 ¼ cup orange marmalade
    1 tablespoon finely chopped cilantro
    1 tablespoon vinegar
    2 tablespoons orange juice
    1 teaspoon Worcestershire sauce
    8 American lamb loin chops, 1 inch thick (about 2 pounds)

For salsa, combine orange, onion, chilies, cranberries, marmalade, cilantro and vinegar in small bowl. Cover; chill several hours. Combine orange juice and Worcestershire. Brush lamb with juice mixture. Grill over medium coals or broil 4 inches from heat source for 5 minutes. Turn and grill or broil 4 to 6 minutes longer or to medium doneness. Serve with salsa.

Makes 4 servings

Favorite recipe from **American Lamb Council**

Texas Beef Brisket

    1 tablespoon paprika
    2 teaspoons salt
    1 teaspoon black pepper
    ¼ teaspoon ground red pepper
   20 ounces beef brisket, trimmed
      Texas BBQ Sauce (recipe follows)

Combine paprika, salt, black and red pepper in small bowl; mix well. Rub spice mixture onto brisket. Cover; marinate in refrigerator overnight.

Prepare Texas BBQ Sauce; set aside. Prepare grill for direct cooking.

Place brisket on grid. Grill, covered, over medium heat 2½ hours or until brisket offers a slight resistance when pierced; check occasionally and baste with sauce as needed. Boil any remaining sauce and serve on the side for dipping. *Makes 4 servings*

Texas BBQ Sauce

   1½ cups ketchup
    ¾ cup honey
    ½ cup cider or white vinegar
    1 small onion, finely chopped
    2 tablespoons Worcestershire sauce
    1 jalapeño pepper,* seeded and minced
    1 tablespoon mustard
    1 teaspoon olive oil

*Jalapeño peppers can sting and irritate the skin; wear rubber gloves when handling peppers and do not touch eyes. Wash hands after handling.

Combine all ingredients; mix well. *Makes about 3 cups*

Memphis Pork Ribs

1 tablespoon chili powder
1 tablespoon dried parsley
2 teaspoons onion powder
2 teaspoons garlic powder
2 teaspoons dried oregano leaves
2 teaspoons paprika
2 teaspoons black pepper
1½ teaspoons salt
4 pounds pork spareribs, cut into 4 racks
Tennessee BBQ Sauce (recipe follows)

Combine chili powder, parsley, onion powder, garlic powder, oregano, paprika, pepper and salt in small bowl; mix well.

Rub spice mixture onto ribs. Cover; marinate in refrigerator at least 2 hours or overnight.

Preheat oven to 350°F. Place ribs in foil-lined shallow roasting pan. Bake 30 minutes.

Meanwhile, prepare grill for direct cooking. Prepare Tennessee BBQ sauce.

Place ribs on grid. Grill, covered, over medium heat 10 minutes. Brush with sauce. Continue grilling 10 minutes or until ribs are tender, brushing with sauce occasionally. *Makes 4 servings*

Tennessee BBQ Sauce

3 cups prepared barbecue sauce
¼ cup cider vinegar
¼ cup honey
2 teaspoons onion powder
2 teaspoons garlic powder
Dash hot pepper sauce

Combine all ingredients in medium bowl; mix well.
Makes about 3½ cups

Memphis Pork Ribs

Ginger Peanut Pork Tenderloin

> 3 tablespoons soy sauce
> 1 tablespoon honey
> 1 tablespoon sesame oil
> 1 tablespoon creamy peanut butter
> 1 tablespoon minced fresh ginger
> 2 teaspoons TABASCO® brand Pepper Sauce
> 1 large clove garlic, minced
> 1 teaspoon curry powder
> ½ teaspoon salt
> 1½ pounds pork tenderloins

Combine all ingredients except pork in medium bowl. Set aside 2 tablespoons mixture. Add pork tenderloins to bowl; cover and marinate at least 2 hours or overnight, turning occasionally.

Preheat grill to medium, placing rack 5 to 6 inches above coals. Place tenderloins on rack; grill 20 to 25 minutes or until no longer pink in center, turning occasionally and brushing frequently with marinade during first 10 minutes of grilling. Let stand 10 minutes before slicing. Brush reserved 2 tablespoons soy sauce mixture over cooked meat.

Makes 6 servings

Barbecued Leg of Lamb

> ⅓ cup A.1.® Steak Sauce
> 2 tablespoons red wine vinegar
> 2 tablespoons vegetable oil
> 1 teaspoon chili powder
> 1 teaspoon dried oregano leaves
> ½ teaspoon coarsely ground black pepper
> ½ teaspoon ground cinnamon
> 2 cloves garlic, crushed
> 1 (5- to 6-pound) leg of lamb, boned, butterflied and trimmed of fat (about 3 pounds after boning)

In small bowl, combine steak sauce, vinegar, oil, chili powder, oregano, pepper, cinnamon and garlic. Place lamb in nonmetal dish; coat with steak sauce mixture. Cover; refrigerate 1 hour, turning occasionally.

Remove lamb from marinade. Grill over medium heat for 25 to 35 minutes or until done, turning often. Cut lamb into thin slices; serve hot.

Makes 12 servings

Seasoned Baby Back Ribs

   1 tablespoon paprika
1½ teaspoons garlic salt
   1 teaspoon celery salt
   ½ teaspoon black pepper
   ¼ teaspoon ground red pepper
   4 pounds pork baby back ribs, cut into 3- to 4-rib portions, well
      trimmed
      Barbecue Sauce (recipe follows)
      Rib rack (optional)
      Orange peel for garnish

1. Preheat oven to 350°F.

2. Combine paprika, garlic salt, celery salt, black pepper and ground red pepper in small bowl. Rub over all surfaces of ribs with fingers.

3. Place ribs in foil-lined shallow roasting pan. Bake 30 minutes.

4. Meanwhile, prepare grill for direct cooking. Prepare Barbecue Sauce; set aside.

5. Transfer ribs to rib rack set on grid. Or, place ribs directly on grid. Grill ribs on covered grill, over medium coals, 10 minutes.

6. Remove ribs from rib rack with tongs; brush with half the Barbecue Sauce evenly over both sides of ribs. Return ribs to rib rack. Continue to grill, covered, 10 minutes or until ribs are tender and browned. Serve with reserved sauce. Garnish, if desired.   *Makes 6 servings*

Barbecue Sauce

   ½ cup ketchup
   ⅓ cup packed light brown sugar
   1 tablespoon cider vinegar
   2 teaspoons Worcestershire sauce
   2 teaspoons soy sauce

Combine ketchup, sugar, vinegar, Worcestershire and soy sauce in glass measuring cup or small bowl. Reserve half of sauce for serving.

Makes about ⅔ cup

Fix It Fast

Grilled Rosemary Chicken

 2 tablespoons lemon juice
 2 tablespoons olive oil
 2 cloves garlic, minced
 2 tablespoons minced fresh rosemary
 ¼ teaspoon salt
 4 boneless skinless chicken breasts

1. Whisk together lemon juice, oil, garlic, rosemary and salt in small bowl. Pour into shallow glass dish. Add chicken, turning to coat both sides with lemon juice mixture. Cover and marinate in refrigerator 15 minutes, turning chicken once.

2. Grill chicken over medium-hot coals 5 to 6 minutes per side or until chicken is no longer pink in center.   *Makes 4 servings*

Cook's Notes: For added flavor, moisten a few sprigs of fresh rosemary and toss on the hot coals just before grilling. Store rosemary in the refrigerator for up to five days. Wrap sprigs in a barely damp paper towel and place in a sealed plastic bag.

Prep and Cook Time: 30 minutes

Hickory Pork Tenderloin with Apple Topping

1¼ cups plus 2 tablespoons LAWRY'S® Hickory Marinade with
    Apple Cider, divided
1 pork tenderloin (2½-3 pounds)
1 can (1 pound 5 ounces) apple pie filling or topping

In large resealable plastic food storage bag, combine 1 cup Hickory Marinade and tenderloin; seal bag. Marinate in refrigerator at least 30 minutes. Remove tenderloin; discard used marinade. Grill tenderloin, using indirect heat method, 35 minutes or until no longer pink in center, turning once and basting often with additional ¼ cup Hickory Marinade. Let stand 10 minutes before slicing. In medium saucepan, combine additional 2 tablespoons Hickory Marinade and apple pie filling. Cook over low heat until heated throughout. Spoon over tenderloin slices. *Makes 6 to 8 servings*

Serving Suggestion: Serve with brussels sprouts and cornbread. Garnish with cranberries, if desired.

Hint: Various flavored applesauces can be substituted for the apple pie filling. Try chunky applesauce with brown sugar and cinnamon.

Hickory Pork Tenderloin with Apple
Topping

Tenderloins with Roasted Garlic Sauce

2 whole garlic bulbs, separated but not peeled (about 5 ounces)
⅔ cup A.1.® Steak Sauce, divided
¼ cup dry red wine
¼ cup finely chopped onion
4 (4- to 6-ounce) beef tenderloin steaks, about 1 inch thick

Place unpeeled garlic cloves on baking sheet. Bake at 500°F for 15 to 20 minutes or until garlic is soft; cool. Squeeze garlic pulp from skins; chop pulp slightly. In small saucepan, combine garlic pulp, ½ cup steak sauce, wine and onion. Heat to a boil; reduce heat and simmer for 5 minutes. Keep warm.

Grill steaks over medium heat for 5 minutes on each side or until done, brushing occasionally with remaining steak sauce. Serve steak with warm garlic sauce.   *Makes 4 servings*

Grilled Tropical Shrimp

¼ cup barbecue sauce
2 tablespoons pineapple juice or orange juice
10 ounces medium shrimp, peeled and deveined
2 medium firm nectarines
6 green onions, cut into 2-inch lengths, or yellow onion wedges

1. Stir together barbecue sauce and pineapple juice. Set aside.

2. Cut each nectarine into 6 wedges. Thread shrimp, nectarines and green onions onto 4 long metal skewers.

3. Spray grill grid with nonstick cooking spray. Prepare grill for direct grilling. Grill skewers over medium coals 4 to 5 minutes or until shrimp are opaque, turning once and brushing frequently with barbecue sauce.
Makes 2 servings

Tip: Although shrimp are high in cholesterol, they are naturally low in total fat and saturated fat, making them a good choice for a low-fat diet.

*Tenderloin with Roasted Garlic
Sauce*

Blue Cheese Stuffed Chicken Breasts

  2 tablespoons butter or margarine, softened, divided
  ½ cup (2 ounces) crumbled blue cheese
  ¾ teaspoon dried thyme leaves
  2 whole boneless chicken breasts with skin (not split)
  1 tablespoon bottled or fresh lemon juice
  ½ teaspoon paprika

1. Prepare grill for direct cooking. Combine 1 tablespoon butter, blue cheese and thyme in small bowl until blended. Season to taste with salt and pepper.

2. Loosen skin over breast of chicken by pushing fingers between skin and meat, taking care not to tear skin. Spread blue cheese mixture under skin with a rubber spatula or small spoon; massage skin to evenly spread cheese mixture.

3. Place chicken, skin side down, on grid over medium coals. Grill over covered grill 5 minutes. Meanwhile, melt remaining 1 tablespoon butter; stir in lemon juice and paprika. Turn chicken; brush with lemon juice mixture. Grill 5 to 7 minutes more or until chicken is cooked through. Transfer chicken to carving board; cut each breast in half.

Makes 4 servings

Serving suggestion: Serve with steamed new potatoes and broccoli.

Mustard-Grilled Red Snapper

  ½ cup Dijon mustard
  1 tablespoon red wine vinegar
  1 teaspoon ground red pepper
  4 red snapper fillets (about 6 ounces each)
  Fresh parsley sprigs and red peppercorns (optional)

Spray grid with nonstick cooking spray. Prepare grill for direct cooking.

Combine mustard, vinegar and pepper in small bowl; mix well. Coat fish thoroughly with mustard mixture.

Place fish on grid. Grill, covered, over medium-high heat 8 minutes or until fish flakes easily when tested with fork, turning halfway through grilling time. Garnish with parsley sprigs and red peppercorns, if desired.

Makes 4 servings

Tempting Taco Burgers

1 envelope LIPTON® RECIPE SECRETS® Onion-Mushroom Soup
    Mix*
1 pound ground beef
½ cup chopped tomato
¼ cup finely chopped green bell pepper
1 teaspoon chili powder
¼ cup water

*Also terrific with LIPTON® RECIPE SECRETS® Onion, Garlic Mushroom, Beefy
Onion or Beefy Mushroom Soup Mix.

1. In large bowl, combine all ingredients; shape into 4 patties.

2. Grill or broil until done. Serve, if desired, on hamburger buns and
top with shredded lettuce and Cheddar cheese.   *Makes 4 servings*

Recipe Tip: The best way to test for doneness of beef, pork, fish and
poultry is to use a meat thermometer or an instant read thermometer.
But, you may want to try this quick touch test first: Gently press a piece
of uncooked flesh to feel what rare feels like; the flesh will become
tighter and more resistant as it cooks. Medium will have some give;
well-done will be quite firm.

Caribbean Jerk Chicken with Quick Fruit Salsa

1 cup plus 2 tablespoons LAWRY'S® Caribbean Jerk Marinade
    with Papaya Juice, divided
1 can (15¼ ounces) tropical fruit salad, drained
4 boneless, skinless chicken breast halves (about 1 pound)

In small glass bowl, combine 2 tablespoons Caribbean Jerk Marinade
and tropical fruit; mix well and set aside. In large resealable plastic food
storage bag, combine additional 1 cup Caribbean Jerk Marinade and
chicken; seal bag. Marinate in refrigerator at least 30 minutes. Remove
chicken; discard used marinade. Grill or broil chicken 10 to 15 minutes
or until no longer pink in center and juices run clear when cut, turning
halfway through grilling time. Top chicken with fruit salsa.

Makes 4 servings

Serving Suggestion: Serve with hot cooked rice and black beans.

Cajun-Style Rubbed Steaks

⅓ cup A.1.® Original or A.1.® BOLD & SPICY Steak Sauce
¼ cup margarine or butter, melted
¾ teaspoon each garlic powder, onion powder and ground black
    pepper
½ teaspoon ground white pepper
¼ teaspoon ground red pepper
4 (4- to 6-ounce) beef shell steaks, about ½ inch thick

In small bowl, blend steak sauce and margarine; set aside.

In another small bowl, combine garlic powder, onion powder and peppers. Brush both sides of steaks with reserved steak sauce mixture, then sprinkle with seasoning mixture. Grill steaks over medium-high heat or broil 4 inches from heat source 5 minutes on each side or to desired doneness. Serve immediately. Garnish as desired.

Makes 4 servings

Grilled Lemon Chicken Dijon

⅓ cup HOLLAND HOUSE® White with Lemon Cooking Wine
⅓ cup olive oil
2 tablespoons Dijon mustard
1 teaspoon dried thyme leaves
2 whole chicken breasts, skinned, boned and halved

Combine all ingredients except chicken in shallow glass baking dish or large resealable plastic food storage bag. Add chicken and turn to coat. Cover or seal bag; marinate in refrigerator 1 to 2 hours.

Prepare grill. Drain chicken, reserving marinade. Grill chicken over medium coals 15 to 20 minutes or until no longer pink in center, turning once and basting with marinade. *(Do not baste during last 5 minutes of grilling.)*

Makes 4 servings

Cajun-Style Rubbed Steak

Thai Grilled Chicken

4 boneless chicken breast halves, skinned if desired
    (about 1¼ pounds)
¼ cup soy sauce
2 teaspoons bottled minced garlic
½ teaspoon red pepper flakes
2 tablespoons honey
1 tablespoon fresh lime juice

1. Prepare grill for direct cooking. Place chicken in shallow dish or plate. Combine soy sauce, garlic and pepper flakes in measuring cup. Pour over chicken, turning to coat. Let stand 10 minutes.

2. Meanwhile, combine honey and lime juice in small bowl until blended; set aside.

3. Place chicken on grid over medium coals; brush with some of marinade remaining in dish. Discard remaining marinade. Grill over covered grill 5 minutes. Brush chicken with half of honey mixture; turn and brush with remaining honey mixture. Grill 5 minutes more or until chicken is cooked through.   *Makes 4 servings*

Serving suggestion: Serve with steamed white rice, Oriental vegetables and fresh fruit salad.

Prep/Cook Time: 25 minutes

Hickory BBQ Chicken

1 can (15 ounces) DEL MONTE® Hickory Sloppy Joe Sauce
¼ cup fresh lime juice
4 boneless skinless chicken breast halves

1. Reserve ½ cup sauce to serve over cooked chicken; cover and refrigerate until 30 minutes before serving. Stir lime juice into remaining sauce in can. Arrange chicken in 11×7-inch dish. Cover with sauce mixture from can; turn to coat. Cover and refrigerate at least 30 minutes or overnight.

2. Grill chicken over hot coals (or broil) 4 minutes per side or until no longer pink in center, brushing chicken occasionally with marinade. Serve with reserved ½ cup sauce. (Any remaining marinade must be boiled for several minutes before serving with chicken.)

Makes 4 servings

Thai Grilled Chicken

Ginger Beef and Pineapple Kabobs

1 cup LAWRY'S® Thai Ginger Marinade with Lime Juice, divided
1 can (16 ounces) pineapple chunks, juice reserved
1½ pounds sirloin steak, cut into 1½-inch cubes
2 red bell peppers, cut into chunks
2 medium onions, cut into wedges

In large resealable plastic food storage bag, combine ½ cup Thai Ginger Marinade and 1 tablespoon pineapple juice; mix well. Add steak, bell peppers and onions; seal bag. Marinate in refrigerator at least 30 minutes. Remove steak and vegetables; discard used marinade. Alternately thread steak, vegetables and pineapple onto skewers. Grill or broil skewers 10 to 15 minutes or until desired doneness, turning once and basting often with additional ½ cup Thai Ginger Marinade. Do not baste during last 5 minutes of cooking. Discard any remaining marinade. *Makes 6 servings*

Serving Suggestion: Serve kabobs with a light salad and bread.

Grilled Salmon Fillets, Asparagus and Onions

½ teaspoon paprika
6 salmon fillets (6 to 8 ounces each)
⅓ cup bottled honey-Dijon marinade or barbecue sauce
1 bunch (about 1 pound) fresh asparagus spears, ends trimmed
1 large red or sweet onion, cut into ¼-inch slices
1 tablespoon olive oil
Salt and black pepper

1. Prepare grill for direct grilling. Sprinkle paprika over salmon fillets. Brush marinade over salmon; let stand at room temperature 15 minutes.

2. Brush asparagus and onion slices with olive oil; season to taste with salt and pepper.

3. Place salmon, skin side down, in center of grid over medium coals. Arrange asparagus spears and onion slices around salmon. Grill salmon and vegetables on covered grill 5 minutes. Turn salmon, asparagus and onion slices. Grill 5 to 6 minutes more or until salmon flakes easily when tested with a fork and vegetables are crisp-tender. Separate onion slices into rings; arrange over asparagus. *Makes 6 servings*

Prep and Cook Time: 26 minutes

Honey-Lime Pork Chops

1 envelope LIPTON® RECIPE SECRETS® Savory Herb with Garlic Soup Mix*
⅓ cup soy sauce
3 tablespoons honey
3 tablespoons lime juice
1 teaspoon grated fresh ginger or ¼ teaspoon ground ginger (optional)
4 pork chops, 1½ inches thick

*Also terrific with LIPTON® RECIPE SECRETS® Garlic Mushroom or Onion Soup Mix.

1. For marinade, blend all ingredients except pork chops.

2. In shallow baking dish or plastic bag, pour ½ cup of the marinade over chops; turn to coat. Cover, or close bag, and marinate in refrigerator, turning occasionally, 2 to 24 hours. Refrigerate remaining marinade.

3. Remove chops from marinade, discarding marinade. Grill or broil chops, turning once and brushing with refrigerated marinade, until chops are done.

Makes 4 servings

Zesty Lemon-Glazed Steak

½ cup A.1.® Original or A.1.® BOLD & SPICY Steak Sauce
2 teaspoons grated lemon peel
1 clove garlic, minced
¼ teaspoon coarsely ground black pepper
¼ teaspoon dried oregano leaves
4 (4- to 6-ounce) beef shell steaks, about ½ inch thick

Blend steak sauce, lemon peel, garlic, pepper and oregano; brush on both sides of steaks. Grill steaks over medium heat or broil 6 inches from heat source 5 minutes on each side or to desired doneness, basting with sauce occasionally. Serve immediately.

Makes 4 servings

Grilled Honey Garlic Pork Chops

¼ cup lemon juice
¼ cup honey
2 tablespoons soy sauce
1 tablespoon dry sherry
2 cloves garlic, minced
4 boneless center-cut lean pork chops (about 4 ounces each)

Combine all ingredients except pork chops in small bowl. Place pork in shallow baking dish; pour marinade over pork. Cover and refrigerate 4 hours or overnight. Remove pork from marinade. Heat remaining marinade in small saucepan over medium heat to a simmer. Grill pork over medium-hot coals 12 to 15 minutes, turning once during cooking and basting frequently with marinade, until meat thermometer registers 155°F to 160°F. *Makes 4 servings*

Favorite recipe from **National Honey Board**

Grilled Steak au Poivre

½ cup A.1.® Steak Sauce, divided
1 (1½-pound) beef sirloin steak, ¾ inch thick
2 teaspoons cracked black pepper
½ cup dairy sour cream
2 tablespoons ketchup

Using 2 tablespoons steak sauce, brush both sides of steak; sprinkle 1 teaspoon pepper on each side, pressing into steak. Set aside.

Blend remaining steak sauce, sour cream and ketchup in medium saucepan. Cook and stir over low heat until heated through (do not boil); keep warm.

Grill steak over medium heat 5 minutes on each side or until done. Serve steak with warm sauce. *Makes 6 servings*

Grilled Honey Garlic Pork Chop

Garlic Skewered Shrimp

1 pound large shrimp, peeled and deveined
2 tablespoons reduced-sodium soy sauce
1 tablespoon vegetable oil
3 cloves garlic, minced
¼ teaspoon red pepper flakes (optional)
3 green onions, cut into 1-inch pieces

Prepare grill or preheat broiler. Soak 4 (12-inch) skewers in water 20 minutes. Meanwhile, place shrimp in large plastic bag. Combine soy sauce, oil, garlic and red pepper in cup; mix well. Pour over shrimp. Close bag securely; turn to coat. Marinate at room temperature 15 minutes.

Drain shrimp; reserve marinade. Alternately thread shrimp and onions onto skewers. Place skewers on grid or rack of broiler pan. Brush with reserved marinade; discard any remaining marinade. Grill, covered, over medium-hot coals, or broil 5 to 6 inches from heat 5 minutes on each side or until shrimp are pink and opaque. Serve on lettuce-lined plate.

Makes 4 servings

Tip: For a more attractive presentation, leave the tails on the shrimp.

Grilled Greek Chicken

1 cup MIRACLE WHIP® Salad Dressing
½ cup chopped fresh parsley
¼ cup dry white wine or chicken broth
1 lemon, sliced and halved
2 tablespoons dried oregano leaves, crushed
1 tablespoon garlic powder
1 tablespoon black pepper
2 (2½- to 3-pound) broiler-fryers, cut up

• Mix together all ingredients except chicken until well blended. Pour over chicken. Cover; marinate in refrigerator at least 20 minutes. Drain marinade; discard.

• Place chicken on grill over medium-hot coals (coals will have slight glow). Grill, covered, 20 to 25 minutes on each side or until tender.

Makes 8 servings

My Favorites

My Favorite Meat Recipes

Favorite recipe: _____

Favorite recipe from: _____

Ingredients: _____

_____

_____

_____

_____

_____

Method: _____

_____

_____

_____

_____

_____

_____

_____

_____

_____

241

My Favorite Meat Recipes

Favorite recipe: _____

Favorite recipe from: _____

Ingredients: _____

_____

_____

_____

_____

_____

Method: _____

_____

_____

_____

_____

_____

_____

_____

_____

_____

My Favorite Meat Recipes

Favorite recipe: _____

Favorite recipe from: _____

Ingredients: _____

_____

_____

_____

_____

_____

Method: _____

_____

_____

_____

_____

_____

_____

_____

_____

_____

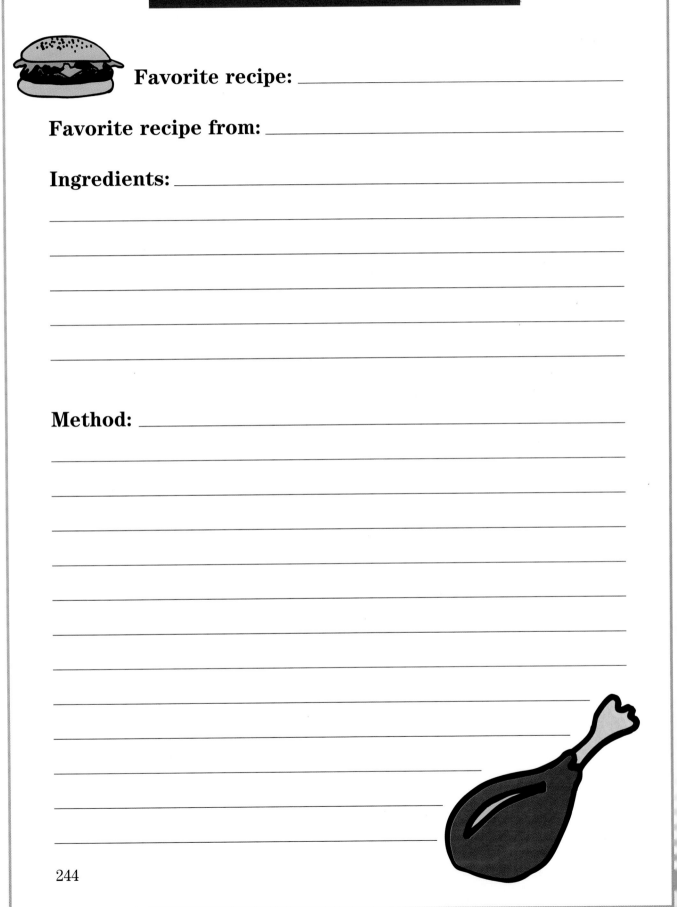

My Favorite Meat Recipes

Favorite recipe: _____

Favorite recipe from: _____

Ingredients: _____

_____

_____

_____

_____

_____

Method: _____

_____

_____

_____

_____

_____

_____

_____

_____

_____

_____

244

My Favorite Meat Recipes

Favorite recipe: _____

Favorite recipe from: _____

Ingredients: _____

_____

_____

_____

_____

_____

Method: _____

_____

_____

_____

_____

_____

_____

_____

_____

_____

_____

My Favorite Meat Recipes

Favorite recipe: _____

Favorite recipe from: _____

Ingredients: _____
_____
_____
_____
_____
_____
_____

Method: _____
_____
_____
_____
_____
_____
_____
_____
_____
_____
_____
_____

My Favorite Meat Recipes

Favorite recipe: _____

Favorite recipe from: _____

Ingredients: _____

_____

_____

_____

_____

_____

Method: _____

_____

_____

_____

_____

_____

_____

_____

_____

_____

_____

My Favorite Meat Recipes

Favorite recipe: _____

Favorite recipe from: _____

Ingredients: _____

_____

_____

_____

_____

_____

Method: _____

_____

_____

_____

_____

_____

_____

_____

_____

_____

_____

My Favorite Meat Recipes

Favorite recipe: _____

Favorite recipe from: _____

Ingredients: _____

_____

_____

_____

_____

_____

Method: _____

_____

_____

_____

_____

_____

_____

_____

_____

_____

_____

Favorite recipe: _____

Favorite recipe from: _____

Ingredients: _____

_____

_____

_____

_____

_____

Method: _____

_____

_____

_____

_____

_____

_____

_____

_____

_____

_____

My Favorite Meat Recipes

Favorite recipe: _____

Favorite recipe from: _____

Ingredients: _____

_____

_____

_____

_____

_____

Method: _____

_____

_____

_____

_____

_____

_____

_____

_____

_____

My Favorite Side Dish Recipes

Favorite recipe: _____

Favorite recipe from: _____

Ingredients: _____

_____

_____

_____

_____

_____

Method: _____

_____

_____

_____

_____

_____

_____

_____

_____

_____

_____

My Favorite Side Dish Recipes

Favorite recipe: _____

Favorite recipe from: _____

Ingredients: _____

_____

_____

_____

_____

_____

Method: _____

_____

_____

_____

_____

_____

_____

_____

_____

_____

_____

253

My Favorite Side Dish Recipes

Favorite recipe: _____

Favorite recipe from: _____

Ingredients: _____

_____

_____

_____

_____

_____

Method: _____

_____

_____

_____

_____

_____

_____

_____

_____

_____

Favorite recipe: _____

Favorite recipe from: _____

Ingredients: _____

_____

_____

_____

_____

_____

_____

Method: _____

_____

_____

_____

_____

_____

_____

_____

_____

_____

_____

_____

Favorite recipe: _____

Favorite recipe from: _____

Ingredients: _____

_____

_____

_____

_____

_____

Method: _____

_____

_____

_____

_____

_____

_____

_____

_____

_____

_____

My Favorite Side Dish Recipes

Favorite recipe: _____

Favorite recipe from: _____

Ingredients: _____

_____

_____

_____

_____

_____

Method: _____

_____

_____

_____

_____

_____

_____

_____

_____

_____

_____

Favorite recipe: _____

Favorite recipe from: _____

Ingredients: _____

_____

_____

_____

_____

_____

Method: _____

_____

_____

_____

_____

_____

_____

_____

_____

_____

My Favorite Side Dish Recipes

Favorite recipe: _____

Favorite recipe from: _____

Ingredients: _____

_____

_____

_____

_____

_____

Method: _____

_____

_____

_____

_____

_____

_____

_____

_____

_____

259

My Favorite Side Dish Recipes

Favorite recipe: _____

Favorite recipe from: _____

Ingredients: _____

_____

_____

_____

_____

_____

Method: _____

_____

_____

_____

_____

_____

_____

_____

_____

_____

_____

260

Favorite recipe: _____

Favorite recipe from: _____

Ingredients: _____

_____

_____

_____

_____

_____

Method: _____

_____

_____

_____

_____

_____

_____

_____

_____

_____

_____

My Favorite Dessert Recipes

Favorite recipe: _____

Favorite recipe from: _____

Ingredients: _____

_____

_____

_____

_____

_____

Method: _____

_____

_____

_____

_____

_____

_____

_____

_____

_____

Favorite recipe: _____

Favorite recipe from: _____

Ingredients: _____

_____

_____

_____

_____

_____

Method: _____

_____

_____

_____

_____

_____

_____

_____

_____

_____

_____

My Favorite Dessert Recipes

Favorite recipe: _____

Favorite recipe from: _____

Ingredients: _____

_____

_____

_____

_____

_____

_____

Method: _____

_____

_____

_____

_____

_____

_____

_____

_____

_____

_____

My Favorite Dessert Recipes

Favorite recipe: _____

Favorite recipe from: _____

Ingredients: _____

_____

_____

_____

_____

_____

_____

Method: _____

_____

_____

_____

_____

_____

_____

_____

_____

_____

_____

My Favorite Dessert Recipes

Favorite recipe: _____

Favorite recipe from: _____

Ingredients: _____

_____

_____

_____

_____

_____

Method: _____

_____

_____

_____

_____

_____

_____

_____

_____

_____

_____

My Favorite Dessert Recipes

Favorite recipe: _____

Favorite recipe from: _____

Ingredients: _____

_____

_____

_____

_____

_____

_____

Method: _____

_____

_____

_____

_____

_____

_____

_____

_____

_____

_____

_____

_____

267

My Favorite Dessert Recipes

Favorite recipe: _____

Favorite recipe from: _____

Ingredients: _____

_____

_____

_____

_____

_____

Method: _____

_____

_____

_____

_____

_____

_____

_____

_____

_____

_____

My Favorite Dessert Recipes

Favorite recipe: _____

Favorite recipe from: _____

Ingredients: _____

_____

_____

_____

_____

_____

Method: _____

_____

_____

_____

_____

_____

_____

_____

_____

_____

_____

_____

_____

269

Favorite recipe: _____

Favorite recipe from: _____

Ingredients: _____

_____

_____

_____

_____

_____

Method: _____

_____

_____

_____

_____

_____

_____

_____

_____

_____

_____

_____

Favorite recipe: _____

Favorite recipe from: _____

Ingredients: _____

_____

_____

_____

_____

_____

_____

Method: _____

_____

_____

_____

_____

_____

_____

_____

_____

_____

_____

_____

My Favorite Dessert Recipes

Favorite recipe: _____

Favorite recipe from: _____

Ingredients: _____

_____

_____

_____

_____

_____

Method: _____

_____

_____

_____

_____

_____

_____

_____

_____

_____

_____

Hints, Tips & Index

THE BASICS

Nothing is more mouthwatering than the smoky aroma of juicy burgers barbecuing outside on a blue-sky summer day...or more satisfying than cutting into a perfectly grilled steak on a starlit night.

By reviewing the following basics, you will soon be grilling like the pros!

BASIC FIRE

• Always place the grill on a solid surface, set away from shrubbery, grass and overhangs.

• NEVER use alcohol, gasoline or kerosene as a lighter fluid starter—all three can cause an explosion.

• To get a sluggish fire going, place two or three additional coals in a small metal can and add lighter fluid. Then, stack them on the coals in the grill and light with a match.

• Keep a water-filled spray bottle near the grill to quench flare-ups.

• Remember: hot coals create a hot grill, grid, tools and food. Always wear heavy-duty fireproof mitts to protect your hands.

• The number of coals required for barbecuing depends on the size and type of grill and the amount of food to be prepared. As a general rule, it takes about 30 coals to grill one pound of meat.

• To light a charcoal fire, arrange the coals in a pyramid shape 20 to 30 minutes prior to cooking. The pyramid shape provides enough ventilation for the coals to catch. To start with lighter fluid, soak the coals with about 1/2 cup lighter fluid. Wait one minute to allow the fluid to soak into the coals, then light with a match.

• To light a charcoal fire using a chimney starter, remove the grid from the grill and place the chimney starter in the base of the grill. Crumble a few sheets of newspaper and place them in the bottom portion of the chimney starter. Fill the top portion with coals. Light the newspaper. The coals should be ready in about 20 to 30 minutes.

• The coals are ready when they are about 80% ash-gray during daylight and glowing at night.

• To lower the cooking temperature, spread the coals farther apart or raise the grid. To raise the cooking temperature, either lower the grid or move the coals closer together and tap off the ash.

CHECKING CHARCOAL TEMPERATURE

A quick, easy way to estimate the temperature of the coals is to hold your hand, palm side down, about 4 inches above the coals. Count the number of seconds you can hold your hand in that position before the heat forces you to pull it away.

Seconds	Coal Temperature
2	hot, 375°F or more
3	medium-hot, 350° to 375°F
4	medium, 300° to 350°F
5	low, 200° to 300°F

BASIC COOKING METHODS

Direct Cooking

The food is placed on the grid directly over the coals. Make sure there is enough charcoal in a single layer to extend 1 or 2 inches beyond the area of the food on the grill. This method is for quick-cooking foods, such as steaks, chops, hamburgers, kabobs and fish.

Indirect Cooking

The food is placed on the grid, over a metal or disposable foil drip pan, with the coals banked either to one side or on both sides of the pan. This method is for slow, even cooking of foods, such as large cuts of meat and whole chickens.

When barbecuing by indirect cooking for more than 45 minutes, extra briquets will need to be added to maintain a constant temperature.

Drugstore Wrap

Place the food in the center of an oblong piece of heavy-duty foil, leaving at least a two-inch border around the food. Bring the two long sides together above the food; fold down in a series of locked folds, allowing for heat circulation and expansion.

Fold the short ends up and over again. Press folds firmly to seal the foil packet.

Grilling Tips

BASIC TIPS

• Always use tongs or a spatula when handling meat. Avoid piercing the meat with a fork.

• Always serve cooked food from the grill on a clean plate, not one that held the raw food.

• The cooking rack, or grid, should be kept clean and free from any bits of charred food. Scrub the grid with a stiff brush while it is still warm.

• Watch foods carefully during grilling. Total cooking time will vary with the type of food, position on the grill, weather, temperature of the coals and the degree of doneness you desire. Set a timer to remind you when it's time to check the food on the grill.

• Store charcoal in a dry place. Charcoal won't burn well if it is damp.

• Top and bottom vents should be open before starting a charcoal grill. Close vents when cooking is finished to extinguish the coals.

• The best way to judge the doneness of meat is with a high-quality meat thermometer. Prior to grilling, insert the thermometer into the thickest part of the meat, not touching any bone. An instant-read thermometer gives an accurate reading within seconds of insertion, although it is not heatproof and should not be left in the meat during grilling.

BASIC TEMPERATURES

This chart gives the basic internal temperatures of meat to determine cooking doneness.

MEAT	DONENESS	TEMPERATURE
Poultry		180°F (170°F in the breast)
Pork		160°F
Beef	Rare	140°F
	Medium-rare	150°F
	Medium	160°F
	Well-done	170°F
Lamb		160°F

Is It Done Yet?

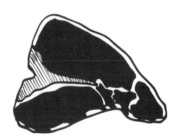

MEAT
  Beef (roast or steak)
    medium—145°F
    well-done—160°F

  Beef (ground)
    cook to 160°F

  Lamb
    medium—145°F
    well-done—160°F

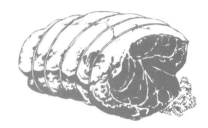

  Pork
    well-done—165°F to 170°F

POULTRY
  Chicken/Turkey
    until temperature in thigh is 180°F
    (whole bird)
    until chicken is no longer pink in
    center
    until temperature in breast is 170°F

SEAFOOD
  Fish
    until fish begins to flake when tested
    with a fork

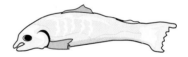

  Shrimp
    until shrimp are pink and opaque

SAUCES
    until (slightly) thickened

VEGETABLES
    until crisp-tender
    until tender
    until browned

Making Marinades & Sauces

• Marinades enhance the flavor of foods, and certain marinades help tenderize tougher cuts of meat.

• Heavy-duty resealable plastic bags are ideal for holding foods as they marinate. Turn marinating foods occasionally to let the flavor infuse evenly.

• Marinate foods in the refrigerator, not at room temperature.

• Marinades can be used as basting and dipping sauces after the food is removed. The marinade first must be boiled for a minimum of 1 minute. This will kill any harmful bacteria that may have contaminated the marinade.

• Basting sauces containing sugar, honey or tomato products should be applied near the end of the grilling process. This will prevent the food from charring.

• Basting sauces made from seasoned oils and butters may be brushed on throughout grilling. Oils and butters prevent leaner cuts of meat from drying out.

Metric Conversion Chart

VOLUME MEASUREMENTS (dry)

1/8 teaspoon = 0.5 mL
1/4 teaspoon = 1 mL
1/2 teaspoon = 2 mL
3/4 teaspoon = 4 mL
1 teaspoon = 5 mL
1 tablespoon = 15 mL
2 tablespoons = 30 mL
1/4 cup = 60 mL
1/3 cup = 75 mL
1/2 cup = 125 mL
2/3 cup = 150 mL
3/4 cup = 175 mL
1 cup = 250 mL
2 cups = 1 pint = 500 mL
3 cups = 750 mL
4 cups = 1 quart = 1 L

VOLUME MEASUREMENTS (fluid)

1 fluid ounce (2 tablespoons) = 30 mL
4 fluid ounces (1/2 cup) = 125 mL
8 fluid ounces (1 cup) = 250 mL
12 fluid ounces (1 1/2 cups) = 375 mL
16 fluid ounces (2 cups) = 500 mL

WEIGHTS (mass)

1/2 ounce = 15 g
1 ounce = 30 g
3 ounces = 90 g
4 ounces = 120 g
8 ounces = 225 g
10 ounces = 285 g
12 ounces = 360 g
16 ounces = 1 pound = 450 g

DIMENSIONS

1/16 inch = 2 mm
1/8 inch = 3 mm
1/4 inch = 6 mm
1/2 inch = 1.5 cm
3/4 inch = 2 cm
1 inch = 2.5 cm

OVEN TEMPERATURES

250°F = 120°C
275°F = 140°C
300°F = 150°C
325°F = 160°C
350°F = 180°C
375°F = 190°C
400°F = 200°C
425°F = 220°C
450°F = 230°C

BAKING PAN SIZES

Utensil	Size in Inches/Quarts	Metric Volume	Size in Centimeters
Baking or Cake Pan (square or rectangular)	8×8×2	2 L	20×20×5
	9×9×2	2.5 L	23×23×5
	12×8×2	3 L	30×20×5
	13×9×2	3.5 L	33×23×5
Loaf Pan	8×4×3	1.5 L	20×10×7
	9×5×3	2 L	23×13×7
Round Layer Cake Pan	8×1½	1.2 L	20×4
	9×1½	1.5 L	23×4
Pie Plate	8×1¼	750 mL	20×3
	9×1¼	1 L	23×3
Baking Dish or Casserole	1 quart	1 L	—
	1½ quart	1.5 L	—
	2 quart	2 L	—

Acknowledgments

**The publisher would like to thank the companies
and organizations listed below for the use of their
recipes and photographs in this publication.**

Almond Board of California

American Lamb Council

A.1.® Steak Sauce

Bestfoods

Bob Evans®

Butterball® Turkey Company

Campbell Soup Company

ConAgra Grocery Products
Company

Del Monte Corporation

Eagle® Brand

Filippo Berio Olive Oil

Fleischmann's® Original Spread

The Golden Grain Company®

Hebrew National®

Hillshire Farm®

Holland House® is a registered
trademark of Mott's, Inc.

The HV Company

Keebler Company

Kikkoman International Inc.

The Kingsford Products
Company

Kraft Foods, Inc.

Lawry's® Foods, Inc.

Lee Kum Kee (USA) Inc.

Lipton®

McIlhenny Company
(TABASCO® brand Pepper
Sauce)

Minnesota Cultivated Wild Rice
Council

Mushroom Council

National Cattlemen's Beef
Association

National Honey Board

National Pork Producers
Council

National Turkey Federation

Nestlé USA, Inc.

Newman's Own, Inc.®

Perdue Farms Incorporated

Reckitt Benckiser

Sargento® Foods Inc.

The Sugar Association, Inc.

Sunkist Growers

Uncle Ben's Inc.

Veg-All®

Washington Apple Commission

Index

Index

Index

Index